101 KEY IDEAS

PSYCHOLOGY

Dave Robinson

D1502799

101 KEY IDEAS

PSYCHOLOGY

Dave Robinson

TEACH YOURSELF BOOKS

For UK orders: please contact Bookpoint Ltd, 78 Milton Park, Abingdon, Oxon OX14 4TD. Telephone: (44) 01235 400414, Fax: (44) 01235 400454. Lines are open from 9.00–6.00, Monday to Saturday, with a 24 hour message answering service. Email address: orders@bookpoint.co.uk

For USA & Canada orders: please contact NTC/Contemporary Publishing, 4255 West Touhy Avenue, Lincolnwood, Illinois 60646–1975, USA. Telephone: (847) 679 5500, Fax: (847) 679 2494.

Long renowned as the authoritative source for self-guided learning – with more than 30 million copies sold worldwide – the *Teach Yourself* series includes over 200 titles in the fields of languages, crafts, hobbies, business and education.

British Library Cataloguing in Publication Data
A catalogue record for this title is available from The British Library.

Library of Congress Catalog Card Number: On file

First published in UK 2000 by Hodder Headline Plc, 338 Euston Road, London, NW1 3BH.

First published in US 2000 by NTC/Contemporary Publishing, 4255 West Touhy Avenue, Lincolnwood (Chicago), Illinois 60646–1975 USA.

The 'Teach Yourself' name and logo are registered trade marks of Hodder & Stoughton Ltd.

Cover design and illustration by Mike Stones

Typeset by Transet Limited, Coventry, England.
Printed in Great Britain for Hodder & Stoughton Educational, a division of Hodder Headline Plc, 338 Euston Road, London NW1 3BH by Cox & Wyman Ltd, Reading, Berkshire.

Impression number	10 9 8 7 6 5 4 3 2
Year	2005 2004 2003 2002 2001 2000

Contents

Introduction

Welcome to the **Teach Yourself 101 Key Ideas** series. We hope that you will find both this book and others in the series to be useful, interesting and informative. The purpose of the series is to provide an introduction to a wide range of subjects, in a way that is entertaining and easy to absorb.

Each book contains 101 short accounts of key ideas or terms which are regarded as central to that subject. The accounts are presented in alphabetical order for ease of reference. All of the books in the series are written in order to be meaningful whether or not you have previous knowledge of the subject. They will be useful to you whether you are a general reader, are on a pre-university course, or have just started at university.

We have designed the series to be a combination of a text book and a dictionary. We felt that many text books are too long for easy reference, while the entries in dictionaries are often too short to provide sufficient detail. The **Teach Yourself 101 Key Ideas** series gives the best of both worlds! Here are books that you do not have to read cover to cover, or in any set order. Dip into them when you need to know the meaning of a term, and you will find a short, but comprehensive account which will be of real help with those essays and assignments. The terms are described in a straightforward way with a careful selection of academic words thrown in for good measure!

So if you need a quick and inexpensive introduction to a subject, **Teach Yourself 101 Key Ideas** is for you. And incidentally, if you have any suggestions about this book or the series, do let us know. It would be great to hear from you.

Best wishes with your studies!

Paul Oliver
Series Editor

Adolescence

Jane looked over at her 12-year-old daughter, Sophie, who was on the telephone to one of her friends. She thought back to Sophie's first day at school – it seemed like yesterday. Sophie was already showing some signs of the onset of puberty. She was growing more quickly and her body shape was changing, but Jane was worried about the psychological changes that might occur during Sophie's adolescent years and the effect that these might have on their relationship.

Jane's concerns are not unusual since adolescence has been described as a period of turmoil, anxiety, storm and stress. It is a period of physical and mental change. The body produces growth and sex hormones that result in accelerated growth and a move towards sexual maturity. In some cases relationships between parents and their adolescent children can become rather tense. However, this phenomenon has probably been exaggerated and the majority of teenagers have good relationships with their parents.

Erik Erikson viewed adolescence as a period of identity formation when teenagers have to make decisions about important issues such as careers, religion and moral codes. Although the process of identity formation doesn't begin or end in adolescence, the search for a sense of identity is particularly important during this period. Individuals who achieve a strong sense of identity after a period of searching for and exploring their identity show a number of positive attributes. They are more autonomous, have a more positive self-concept and have good relationships with their parents.

On the whole, adolescents tend to spend less time with their families and more time with friends and peers than they did as children. Although it is clear that being a member of a peer group results in pressure to behave in certain ways, it is also the case that adolescents seek out groups that match most closely their own characteristics.

see also...

Attachment; Cognitive Development; Social Development; Moral Development

Ageing

t has been suggested that we spend about one-quarter of our lives growing up and three-quarters growing old! Adult ageing is a complex process involving social, cognitive and biological change. By the time we are in our twenties we are already experiencing a net loss of brain cells, a process which will continue to accelerate throughout the rest of our lives. Many people now live well past their seventieth birthday and it is anticipated that the majority of today's college students will enjoy their eightieth birthday. But what effect does growing old have on our cognitive processes and our social relationships?

In terms of our relationships with others, one view is that as we grow older people become more concerned with enjoying the present and are less likely to invest time and effort on developing new friendships. Existing relationships with partners, close friends and family will tend to grow stronger and become more valued. Changes are evident in the workplace as well, with older workers enjoying work more than younger workers. It is likely that this reflects older workers' emphasis on positive aspects of the present and a relative lack of concern about future career progression.

Many modern societies force people to retire at an arbitrary age of, for example, 65. However, it has been suggested that society should focus on individuals' actual capacities and abilities, their functional age, rather than their chronological age. There is some evidence that this view is held in the political arena where older people can make a significant impact and hold influential positions. For example, Nelson Mandela became President of South Africa at the age of 75.

Not everybody experiences later life in the same way since personality, physical factors and financial factors can all play a significant role in the way that people adjust as they get older. The old adage 'use it or lose it' seems to apply to cognitive as well as physical abilities. Fewer cognitive declines are observed in people who remain intellectually active than those who don't.

see also...

Attachment; Cognitive Development; Dementia; Social Development

Aggression

James is late for an important meeting. He is driving along a narrow road and a tractor pulls out in front of him and slows him down. James starts honking his horn and shouting at the driver of the tractor. When the tractor pulls over James stops the car and jumps out to continue shouting at the driver. Why is James behaving in such an aggressive manner?

Within psychology there are a number of different theories which have attempted to explain aggression. The original version of the frustration-aggression theory suggests that when people's attempts to achieve a goal are frustrated it leads to aggressive behaviour. However, frustration doesn't always lead to aggression. Many people in James's situation would simply resign themselves to being late for the meeting. A more recent version of the frustration-aggression theory proposes that events which we find unpleasant cause negative feelings which in turn can predispose people to behave aggressively. An alternative account of aggressive behaviour is provided by Freud's psychodynamic approach which sees

aggression as a basic human instinct. Unlike other approaches, a psychodynamic perspective argues that all humans find aggression pleasurable to some extent. However, the psychodynamic emphasis on aggression, as something that emerges from within the person, underplays the role of situational factors in determining aggressive behaviour.

Social learning theories argue that aggression is a learned behaviour. These theories propose that children and adults can learn to be aggressive by observing aggression in other people. One problem with social learning theories is that not everyone is influenced by the behaviour of others in the same way. Whether we end up behaving aggressively or not depends on a number of factors including our thought processes and biology, as well as our previous learning experiences.

see also...

Brain Structure; Freud, Sigmund; Moral Development; Pro-Social Behaviour; Psychodynamic Approaches

Anxiety and Anxiety Disorders

It's holiday time. You are with your family on the plane, final preparations have been completed and the cabin crew are seated ready for take off. As you check your seat belt you might notice some physical reactions such as your heart rate increasing and your palms becoming a little sweaty. You might also start to worry and think about recent reports of air crashes. Some people experience similar symptoms when visiting the dentist for a check-up or making a speech to a large number of people. These physical changes and thoughts are part of our body's response to potentially threatening situations that we face in our everyday lives. We use the term anxiety to describe this combination of thoughts and physical symptoms.

If the levels of anxiety become extreme then the person can be said to be suffering from an anxiety disorder. Approximately 15 per cent of the US population suffer from an anxiety disorder at some time during their lives.

There are five main types of anxiety disorder: phobia; panic disorder; obsessive-compulsive disorder; generalized anxiety disorder and post-traumatic stress disorder. In a phobia there is usually a specific focus for the anxiety such as snakes or spiders. Panic disorder is characterized by extreme physical reactions including shortness of breath and dizziness and the person often thinks they are going to die or have a heart attack. Generalized anxiety disorder doesn't have the same kind of specific aspects to it, rather the person experiences persistently high levels of anxiety across a wide range of situations. Post-traumatic stress disorder occurs as a result of the person experiencing an extremely distressing event and is associated with flashbacks, nightmares and an inability to stop thinking about the event. Obsessive-compulsive disorder is marked by an extreme preoccupation with a perceived danger (obsession) and a repetitive behaviour carried out to avoid the danger (compulsion).

see also...

Behaviour Therapy; Clinical Psychology; Cognitive-Behavioural Therapy; Depression; Post-Traumatic Stress Disorder

Asch, Solomon

It is lunchtime at work and you are sitting with colleagues talking about a film you all watched on television the previous night. You thought the film was mediocre and boring, but it soon becomes clear that everyone else thought the film was excellent. The person next to you turns and says, 'You haven't told us what you thought about the film. What do you think Chris?' How would you respond? Would you go along with the majority even though it wasn't what you really thought? Have your colleagues seen something about the film that you missed? Can all these people really be wrong?

However you responded, the chances are you would have found it difficult and probably stressful. One of Solomon Asch's enduring contributions to psychology is a series of classic studies he carried out in the 1950s. These studies demonstrated very clearly the extent to which people find it difficult to disagree with the majority view. In a typical experiment he asked groups of people to make a decision about which of three lines was the same length as a standard line. Asch would hold up a card with one line on it (the standard line); he would then hold up another card with three lines labelled A, B and C. People in the group had to decide which of these lines most closely matched the standard line. An easy enough task you might think, but the twist was that in each case only one member of the group was a research participant; the rest of the group were actors being paid by Asch to give predetermined answers, some of which were wrong.

In situations where the rest of the group gave the wrong answer, about 37 per cent of the research participants conformed and went along with the majority and also gave the wrong answer. It is interesting to note that despite the fact that in Asch's experiments the only pressure to conform came from the 'wrong' answers given by the actors, a significant number of people were not able to resist the power of the group. Asch's experiments demonstrate how difficult it is for us to disagree openly with other people.

see also...

Cognitive Dissonance; Groups; Milgram, Stanley; Social Psychology

Attachment

Helen is two years old and is sitting on the floor playing with her toys. Her mother, Julia, has an old school friend over whom she hasn't seen for several years and they are chatting about old times. Julia goes to the kitchen to make coffee while her friend keeps an eye on Helen. When Julia leaves the room Helen looks a little upset and when Julia returns Helen moves towards her mother and grabs hold of her leg. They have a hug and Helen returns to playing with her toys and Julia continues to chat with her friend.

This scenario resembles the 'Strange Situation' technique developed by Margaret Ainsworth to assess children's attachment. The technique involves the parent leaving the child with a stranger for a couple of minutes and then returning to the room. When the parent returns, the child's behaviour is used to assess the child's attachment to the parent. Attachments are categorized broadly as either secure or insecure. Helen's behaviour is characteristic of a secure attachment. She is mildly upset at the departure of her mother but is easily comforted when Julia returns. Three types of insecure attachment have been identified. The first of these is 'avoidant' where the child typically ignores and avoids the parent when they return. The second is 'resistant', when the child would typically alternate between clinging to the parent and pushing them away. The final type is 'disorganized' which contains elements of both avoidant and resistant as well as behaviour which suggests fear and confusion.

It was John Bowlby, a British psychiatrist, who proposed that the interaction between caregiver and child led to the formation of an emotional bond or attachment between them. All children appear to form an attachment with their caregiver and most children develop attachments with fathers as well as mothers. The nature of this attachment is seen as having a particularly important influence on their subsequent development.

see also...

*Cognitive Development;
Developmental Psychology;
Gender Development; Social
Development*

Attitudes

Nigel and Mary have invited some friends around for a drink. Nigel and Bill are sorting out the country's problems. Nigel says, 'Drugs are a major cause of social problems in our country. Drugs are really bad! There is no way I am ever doing drugs.' Mary and Elaine are discussing the merits of various cosmetics. Mary says, 'Using skin care products slows down the ageing process. You know, skin care products are a really good idea. I use them all the time.' These are examples of people expressing attitudes. An attitude is a tendency to express a negative or positive evaluation of a person, object or a set of ideas.

Traditionally, psychologists have viewed attitudes as comprising three components: a belief (drugs cause social problems, skin care products slow down ageing); an evaluative component (drugs are bad, skin products are good); and a disposition to behave in a particular way (don't do drugs, use skin care products). But is a person's behaviour always consistent with their beliefs? We need only to look at smoking behaviour to realize that this is not the case. Millions of people continue to smoke despite knowing that it damages their health.

There are a number of factors that can influence the relationship between beliefs and behaviour. First, how the belief is acquired is important, since beliefs based on direct experience are more likely to be expressed than those acquired second hand. Secondly, the views of those we consider important to us, such as parents and best friends, can have a significant impact on the way in which people behave. If you think these important people in your life would approve of your behaviour you would be more likely to do it than if you thought they would disapprove of the behaviour. Thirdly, a person's evaluation of the consequences of carrying out a particular behaviour can influence whether or not they actually do something. Finally, if a person anticipates feeling bad or regretting their actions, they are less likely to do it than if they anticipate feeling good about it.

see also...

Cognitive Dissonance; Impression Formation; Prejudice; Stereotypes

Attribution

You are driving along a straight country road, the weather is dry although there has been a little rain on and off throughout the day so the road is damp. A car starts to overtake but something goes wrong. The car skids and ends up in the ditch. Why did the accident happen? You are at work and ask a colleague a question. You get a rude and unhelpful reply. Why did your colleague respond that way? Whether we are trying to make sense of an accident or the unhelpful response of a colleague, we are constantly engaged in making inferences about the causes of behaviours and events. This is the process of making attributions, where an attribution is a person's belief about the cause of an event or behaviour.

In most cases it is possible to attribute the cause of an event to the situation, the person, or an interaction between the two. There are a number of biases which affect the attributions that people make. These include the 'fundamental attribution error' which refers to the tendency to overestimate the role of the person and underestimate the impact of the situation. So in the first example, people would tend to attribute the cause of the accident to the driver – he or she was driving too fast, and/or not paying attention – rather than to the road conditions or a mechanical failure. In the second example there would be a tendency to see your colleague simply as a rude person, whereas, in fact, the rudeness could be a reflection of his high stress levels due to an abnormally heavy workload or a crisis in his personal life. Another bias has been called the 'self-serving bias'. This refers to the tendency to attribute one's successes to oneself whereas failures are attributed to external factors. So if you pass your driving test first time you will tend to attribute this to your driving skills, whereas if you fail it is likely to be attributed to the traffic conditions or a harsh examiner!

see also...

Attitudes; Cognitive Dissonance; Impression Formation; Social Psychology

8

Autism

Nathan is nine years old. In school he has no friends and shows little interest in making any. He has no sense of humour and is unable to share a joke with the other pupils in his class. At home he has a small collection of trains with doors that open and close. Nathan shows little interest in using the trains in imaginative or pretend play. He would rather spend his time opening and closing the doors. At bedtime he becomes very upset and angry if the curtains in his room are not exactly 25 cm apart. There are similar problems at lunchtime if his food isn't served in a particular bowl. When Nathan does communicate, his sentences are very short and he speaks only in response to questions. Nathan was diagnosed as autistic at the age of three.

Autistic children have a strong desire to maintain the same routines and are resistant to change. The main characteristics of autism are: difficulties in social interaction, problems with language and non-verbal communication; and a restricted range of interests – all of which are present before the child is three years of age. In most cases autism is a lifelong condition, although the pattern and severity of the difficulties may change as the person gets older. Autism occurs in approximately four children in every 10,000. There are about three times as many males diagnosed with autism as females.

Psychologists have attempted to identify the reasons why some children become autistic. Evidence from studies looking at the incidence of autism in identical twins suggests that there is a genetic component to its development. Other studies have looked for differences in the brain structure of children with autism. Some of these studies have found abnormalities in the brains of children with autism, for example, one study reported an abnormality in the part of the brain called the cerebellum. But as yet, the relationship between brain structure and autism remains unclear.

see also...

Clinical Psychology; Developmental Psychology; Dyslexia; Non-Verbal Communication; Social Development

Bandura, Albert

Albert Bandura was born in Canada in 1925. He was awarded a doctorate in 1952 from the University of Iowa and shortly afterwards he took up a teaching position at Stanford University. Throughout his career Bandura has been interested in developing theories of learning and personality. One of his major contributions to psychology has been the development of his 'Social Learning Theory.'

Much of Bandura's early work focused on the extent to which people can learn by observing the behaviour of others. In one of his early studies he used a large inflatable doll called Bobo. Groups of children watched an adult interacting with the doll in different ways. One group saw the adult attacking the doll, both verbally and physically, while another group observed the adult behaving in a non-violent manner with the doll. The children were then left alone with the Bobo doll and observed to see if they expressed any aggressive behaviour towards it. It was found that the children who had observed the aggressive behaviour were more likely to display aggressive behaviour themselves. So it would appear that one of the ways in which children learn is through the observation of others.

In the example above, the manner in which the adult interacted with the Bobo doll had neither negative nor positive consequences. What would be the effect on the children if they saw the adult being punished or rewarded as a consequence of their interaction with the doll? Bandura's research suggests that the children would be more likely to demonstrate aggressive behaviours with the doll if they had observed the adult being rewarded as a result of their aggressive actions towards the doll, rather than observing the adult being reprimanded for displaying aggressive behaviour. The process of learning the consequences of a behaviour by observing its consequences for someone else is referred to as vicarious conditioning.

see also...

Aggression; Conditioning; Skinner, Burrhus F.; Social Psychology

Behaviour Modification

Andrew is an eight-year-old boy who is exhibiting disruptive behaviour in the classroom. He finds it very difficult to remain seated for more than a couple of minutes and persists in interfering with the work of other pupils. Every time he does this his teacher tells him to sit down and get on with his own work, but while he is sitting down his teacher pays him little attention. His teacher discusses the problem with an educational psychologist and Andrew's parents. They agree to try a behaviour modification programme.

Behaviour modification is specifically aimed at changing behaviour; it is not concerned with the relationship between the person's thoughts and feelings and their behaviour. It is based on the principles of operant conditioning (also referred to as instrumental conditioning) which were developed by Burrhus F. Skinner.

Skinner observed that you can increase the likelihood of a behaviour occurring if you ensure that the behaviour is followed by a reward or positive reinforcement such as food or praise. The first stage in the development of a behaviour modification programme for Andrew would be a careful analysis of the situations in which he was behaving appropriately and those in which he was behaving disruptively. For example, in Andrew's case the fact that his teacher paid attention to him when he was standing up might actually be reinforcing the disruptive behaviour. A behaviour modification programme would aim to build up appropriate behaviours, for example, staying seated, by the use of reinforcers such as praise. Whereas the disruptive behaviour would be extinguished by ensuring that it went unrewarded.

Behaviour modification has formed the basis of 'token economies' which have been used extensively in a variety of institutions such as hospitals. People are given tokens, for example, gold stars, in return for exhibiting appropriate behaviour.

see also...

Behaviour Therapy; Behaviourism; Cognitive-Behavioural Therapy; Conditioning; Skinner, Burrhus F.

Behaviour Therapy

William is a six-year-old with a bed-wetting problem. Unfortunately, a couple of nights every week William wets the bed without waking. This is causing a number of problems within the family. William's clinical psychologist suggests that they try using the 'bell and pad' method. This entails placing a water sensitive pad in William's bed. The pad is connected to a bell that rings when the pad becomes wet, so every time William starts to urinate in his sleep the alarm will go off and wake him up. The aim of this is to enable William to associate the sensations of discomfort in his bladder muscles with waking up. In other words, William is pairing a stimulus (bodily sensation of a full bladder) with a response (waking up). The type of learning that involves associating stimulus with a response is called classical conditioning. Behaviour therapy is also used to help people extinguish learned responses.

In the case of people with phobias, such as an excessive fear of spiders, a technique called systematic desensitization is often used. It usually starts with the person suffering from the phobia being taught relaxation techniques. Once the person is familiar with the relaxation techniques and is able to use them effectively the object of the phobia is gradually introduced. If the phobia is a fear of spiders the therapy might start with a picture of a spider, or even the word 'spider'. It is important that the person is able to use the relaxation training in order that they feel calm and relaxed during the presentation of the object of their phobia. The severity of the stimulus is gradually increased in stages. For example, the picture of a spider might be followed by a plastic spider and then, eventually, a real spider would be used. Systematic desensitization aims to gradually replace the response of fear and anxiety associated with the spider (stimulus) with an alternative response, a state of relaxation.

---

see also...

Anxiety; Behaviour Modification; Behaviourism; Clinical Psychology; Conditioning; Cognitive-Behavioural Therapy; Skinner, Burrhus F.

Behaviourism

You are seated on a bench in the park. A dog walks by and you reach out to stroke it and the dog bites you. You feel upset and shaken up by the event. A couple of weeks later you are at friend's house and a dog comes running towards you. You have the same feelings of upset as you experienced in the park. Students of behaviourism would argue that your reaction is the result of an association forming between a stimulus (the dog) and a response (feeling upset). So the presence of a dog at your friend's house elicits the same response.

Behaviourism is an approach to psychology that developed in the United States in the early part of the twentieth century. Prior to the advent of behaviourism much psychological research relied on the 'introspective method' which required individuals to report on their own thought processes. John B. Watson (1878–1958) argued strongly that introspection was fundamentally flawed since it wasn't possible to establish the accuracy of reports gathered using this method. Instead, Watson proposed that we should focus on observable behaviour and believed that eventually we would be able to explain all human behaviour in terms of stimulus-response associations.

Building on the work of Watson and other behaviourists Burrhus F. Skinner developed an approach that emphasized the role of reinforcement in behaviour. Skinner argued that when a reward (positive reinforcement) is given after a behaviour has been exhibited, it increases the likelihood of the behaviour occurring again. For example, praising and encouraging the hard work of students is a form of positive reinforcement in the classroom that is likely to increase the probability of them working hard in the future.

see also...

Behaviour Modification; Behaviour Therapy; Cognitive-Behavioural Therapy; Conditioning; Skinner, Burrhus F.

Biopsychology

Biopsychology is concerned with the relationship between biological processes operating in the body and behaviour. Although biopsychologists recognize the fact that human behaviour is influenced by a number of factors, such as our past experiences and the behaviour of other people, their research focuses primarily on biological processes. Consider the behaviour of Alex who has spent most of the morning shopping for a new suit without any success. He decides he needs a break and goes into a café where he orders a large coffee and a slice of apple pie. Why does he order the food? One explanation could be that the effort that Alex has expended in walking around looking for a suit has depleted his energy reserves. This is the traditional view of hunger. According to this view we are driven to find food and restore our body's functioning to a balanced state. But seeing eating as a behaviour simply aimed at reducing a physiological need doesn't seem to match with our everyday experiences. For example, Alex might not be hungry and has ordered the apple pie simply because it tastes good!

Biopsychologists have identified three factors that are implicated in the control of food intake at meal times. First, the fact that the stomach swells after eating and then gradually contracts as the food is digested provides the basis for one mechanism. There is a nerve pathway from the stomach to the brain which provides information on the extent to which the stomach is full or empty. Second, as food passes from the stomach it stimulates the release of a substance called cholecystokinin (CCK). CCK enters the bloodstream and appears to have the function of telling the body to stop eating. Third, the appearance, taste, texture and smell of the food can influence how much we eat.

Biopsychologists are also interested in the biological changes that are associated with many other psychological phenomena such as learning, memory and emotion.

see also...

Brain Structure; Emotion; Neurons; Neurotransmitters; Sleep; Stress

Brain Structure

I f you were able to take your brain out of your skull and inspect it, the first thing to strike you would be the wrinkled appearance of its outer layer. It looks rather like an oversized walnut that has been carefully taken out of its shell. This outer layer is called the cerebral cortex. Some areas of the cortex have developed to support specialized roles. There is a region at the rear of the cortex referred to as the visual cortex which deals with information that comes via our eyes. The front of the cortex, the frontal lobes, appears to be the part of our cortex involved in planning our future actions and behaviour. Midway between the visual cortex at the rear of our brain and the frontal lobes, is the motor cortex which is responsible for controlling movement. Different parts of the motor cortex are associated with different parts of our body, so there are areas in the motor cortex that are responsible for controlling the movement of our legs, arms, fingers, face and so on.

The brain is more or less symmetrical and is composed of two identical halves, a left and a right hemisphere. The two hemispheres communicate with each other by means of a bundle of nerve cells called the corpus callosum. Although the two hemispheres are almost identical to look at they are, in fact, specialized for different kinds of activity. For example, language is primarily, although not exclusively, dealt with by the left hemisphere, whereas spatial processing, such as recognizing three-dimensional objects, is carried out in the right hemisphere.

The cerebral cortex envelops numerous other brain structures including the thalamus. Most of the input from sensory organs, such as the eyes, nose, and ears, passes through the thalamus which then relays the information to the appropriate part of the brain. Underneath the thalamus and toward the front of the brain is a small structure called the hypothalamus which is involved in regulating emotions and our responses to stressful situations.

see also...

Biopsychology; Comparative Psychology; Neurons; Neurotransmitters; Stress

Chomsky, Noam

'Christine is stroking the cat.' Christine likes cats so this is an event that happens on a regular basis in her house! The same event could be described using the following sentence: 'The cat is being stroked by Christine.' Both these sentences have the same meaning but are structured in different ways. Noam Chomsky developed a theory of language that made explicit the difference between the actual words and sentences we hear and the meanings that underlie the sentences. The idea that we can distinguish between 'surface structure' and 'deep structure' can be illustrated in ambiguous sentences that have identical surface structures but can have different deep structures depending on the context. For example, 'They were cooking apples' could refer to a type of apple or a group of people engaged in the process of making apple pie! The two possible meanings of this ambiguous sentence reflect different underlying deep structures.

Chomsky developed a complex system called 'transformational grammar' which demonstrated how it is possible to transform the deep structure into the surface structure we recognize and use as sentences. Chomsky went on to argue that this deep structure is based on a set of underlying principles that is common to all human language. His views on the way in which children acquire language was fundamentally at odds with the account presented by the influential behaviourist psychologist, Burrhus F. Skinner.

According to Chomsky children are born with an innate ability to acquire language. He used the term 'language acquisition device' to describe the set of inborn brain structures that are responsible for the acquisition of language. On the other hand, Skinner argued that we acquire language through a process of trial and error and reinforcement of particular sounds. For example, Skinner suggests that adults respond to the vocalizations of young babies when the sounds are similar to the ones they use in their own language.

see also...

Behaviourism; Cognitive Development; Language; Language Acquisition; Skinner, Burrhus F.

Chronic Illness

hronic illness has been defined as an irreversible physical condition, which lasts for more than three months in a given year and often involves regular visits to a hospital. It has been estimated that chronic illness affects approximately 10-15 per cent of children and up to 30 per cent of adults. The most common chronic illness in childhood is asthma, and as people get older, problems such as heart disease, arthritis, multiple sclerosis and diabetes increase in prevalence.

One psychological model of chronic illness proposes that our understanding of an illness develops in four stages. The first stage is one of uncertainty when patients attempt to understand the meaning and severity of their symptoms. The second stage is characterized by a crisis as it becomes clear to patients that they are suffering from a serious illness. Patients typically show high levels of stress and require considerable support from family and friends, as well as health care professionals. In the third stage patients attempt to gain some form of control over their illness and rely on various forms of coping behaviour. In the final stage patients have adapted to the situation and have come to accept the illness and its consequences.

A person's level of self-efficacy appears to play an important role in determining whether or not he or she adapts effectively to chronic illness and pain. People with relatively high levels of self-efficacy not only cope better with their illness but also report lower levels of pain and less severe physical symptoms. Psychological interventions in chronic illness are primarily aimed at enhancing people's quality of life and in helping them to manage their illness in the most effective way. Interventions can include physical training programmes, counselling, social skills training and stress management programmes.

see also...

Coping Strategies; Health Psychology; Psychotherapy; Self-Efficacy; Stress

Clinical Psychology

When James thinks about going outside his house he starts to feel tense, his mouth gets dry, he starts to sweat and tremble. These are the symptoms commonly associated with agoraphobia, a fear of being alone in public places. Amanda is 24 years old. She was abused as a child and is now finding it very difficult to maintain relationships. Amanda also has low self-esteem and believes that she is a worthless person. Both Amanda and James are experiencing the kinds of difficulties which clinical psychologists are trained to deal with. As well as promoting psychological health in individuals, clinical psychology is also concerned with families, groups and organizations.

Clinical psychologists help people with learning difficulties to develop the skills they need to care for themselves. They also work with people who have eating disorders, sexual problems, phobias, head injuries, strokes, HIV/AIDS, and problems associated with age. They usually work directly with clients, either individually or in groups, assessing their needs and providing therapies based on psychological theories and research. Clinical psychologists draw on a wide range of assessment and intervention techniques in order to alleviate the discomforts encountered by their clients. The main purpose of the assessment is to identify the causes of the problems currently being experienced by their clients. Interviews are one of the most common methods used during assessment. Other commonly used methods include administering and interpreting tests of intellectual ability, aptitudes and personal characteristics, and carrying out behavioural assessments to identify why particular behaviours are occurring.

Clinical psychologists work in a variety of settings, including health centres, hospitals, military services and private practice. In many countries, for example in the United Kingdom, clinical psychologists usually work as part of a team with other health professionals, medical practitioners and social workers.

see also...

Anxiety; Depression; Psychological Tests; Schizophrenia

Cognitive-Behavioural Therapy

Cognitive-behavioural therapy is one of the major approaches used in the treatment of mental health problems such as depression and anxiety. It draws on methods from behavioural and cognitive approaches. Cognitive therapies assume that distortions in a person's thoughts and beliefs (cognitions) can lead to a number of mental health problems including depression and anxiety.

One of the best known cognitive approaches to therapy has been developed by Aaron Beck. Based on observations of patients with depression, Beck suggested that distorted thought processes can result in people having a negative view of themselves, their future and the world in general. He proposed that this pessimistic style of thinking is responsible for producing and maintaining depression. For example, Maureen is a journalist who is very competent at her job, but recently she has been feeling a bit down about life in general. She has just completed a big story that she has been working on for a couple of days and has given it to her editor. The editor tells her that it is a really good article but that it could be improved by making some relatively minor alterations. Maureen is devastated by this news. It confirms her view that the article is rubbish and she is useless, worthless and can't do anything right. Maureen is demonstrating two types of distorted thinking. First, she is focusing on the negative part of her editor's message and ignoring the fact that he said it was a really good article. Secondly, she is making generalizations, about herself as a person, on the basis of very limited information. These types of distorted thinking are characteristic of people with depression.

An important feature of Beck's theory is that he suggests that it is not the event itself which is responsible for causing the depression, but rather the way in which the person interprets the event. During cognitive therapy the therapist will help clients identify their negative thoughts and will challenge them.

see also...

Anxiety; Behaviour Therapy; Clinical Psychology; Depression; Psychotherapy

Cognitive Development

Four-year-old Wayne is in the kitchen helping his father with the cooking. Wayne has a bowl, flour and some water and is trying to copy his father who is making bread. 'It's not working!' He shouts to his father. 'It goes too sloppy or too dry.' His father tries to explain. 'OK. So what you have to do if it's too sloppy is to sprinkle a little flour in, mix it up for a while and see how it goes. If it's too dry you keep adding water, a little bit at a time, until you get it right.' It doesn't seem to matter how his father tries to explain it, Wayne doesn't seem to be able to understand that it is the ratio of flour to water that is important. He continues putting in either too much water or too much flour. Why is it hard for Wayne to understand something that seems so simple for an adult? This is the kind of question asked by psychologists who are interested in cognitive development. They are concerned with the ways in which intellectual abilities develop throughout childhood and into adulthood.

There are a number of different explanations that could be offered to account for Wayne's inability to grasp the notion of combining flour and water in the correct proportions. Jean Piaget, who saw child development as comprising a series of stages, would argue that Wayne hadn't reached the stage in his development where he can think in terms of quantities. Another explanation could be Wayne's lack of experience with mixing solids and liquids. He needs to acquire more experience through practice. Children's cognitive skills develop at an amazing rate from birth onwards. As soon as they are born babies are capable of distinguishing between different sounds and of recognizing their mother's voice. Vision is less well developed at birth, but even babies less than an hour old are capable of copying the facial movements of adults, such as sticking the tongue out or opening the mouth. As they get older, children's knowledge of the world develops and they become more able to plan and apply their knowledge to new situations.

see also...

Developmental Psychology; Language Development; Moral Development; Piaget, Jean; Social Development

Cognitive Dissonance

Marie is a vegetarian. She believes killing animals, even for food, is wrong. Marie and her husband, Alan, are on holiday in Spain and they make friends with some other holidaymakers who persuade them to see a bullfight. Their new friends argue that bullfighting is part of the cultural heritage of Spain and it's something they shouldn't miss. When Marie is seated in the arena she begins to worry if she has made the right choice. Marie is experiencing a discrepancy between her attitudes towards animals and her current behaviour. This discrepancy is referred to as cognitive dissonance.

According to Leon Festinger, people have a basic need to be consistent in their beliefs. One of the consequences of a discrepancy is a state of tension and psychological discomfort. The discomfort Marie is experiencing is called post-decision regret. She might try to reduce it by telling herself that she is here only to find out more about bullfighting so she will be in a better position to criticize it when it crops up in future conversations. In other words, she is attempting to justify a choice that is inconsistent with her choice to be a vegetarian. Attitude change is another way to reduce cognitive dissonance. For example, Marie could change her attitude towards killing animals.

In a classic piece of research into cognitive dissonance people were paid either $1 or $20 to complete a boring task and then tell the next person in line that the task was really enjoyable. The interesting finding was that the people who were paid $1 rated the task as more enjoyable than those who were paid $20. The explanation of this in terms of cognitive dissonance is that people who received only $1 experienced considerable dissonance and had either to change their attitudes towards the task or admit that they were exploited in terms of performing a boring task for little reward. People tended to modify their view of the task and see it as less boring than it really was.

see also...

Attitudes; Attribution; Motivation; Social Psychology

Cognitive Psychology

Cognitive psychology is concerned with the study of mental processes, in particular the ways in which people process, store, and retrieve information. These mental processes are collectively referred to as cognition. Imagine the following scenario. Imran is walking down the street. He looks at the cars coming towards him and recognizes a red Corvette belonging to one of his friends. He waves and continues his walk to work. When he arrives at the office he walks across to the elevator where his colleague is standing. 'Hi John.' 'Hi Imran. Did you see the basketball game on the television last night? It was one of the best games I've ever seen.' Imran replies, 'No, I missed it. I was visiting relatives.'

We can use Imran's journey to work to illustrate three topics that are of interest to cognitive psychologists: perception, language and memory. Perception is concerned with the way in which we extract information from the environment. For example, visual perception is concerned with the processes involved in the transformation of the pattern of light which enters Imran's eyes into the three-dimensional representation which enables him to recognize the car as his friend's red Corvette. Cognitive psychologists are concerned with processes involved in the production and comprehension of both spoken and written language. For example, how does Imran understand what John says to him and how does he produce his reply? From a cognitive perspective, memory is concerned with the encoding, storage and retrieval of information. For example, what are the factors that influence Imran's recall? Why does Imran not remember everything?

There are no simple answers to any of these questions. Most cognitive psychologists think the route to a better understanding of these processes is by carrying out carefully controlled experimental research.

see also...

*Developmental Psychology;
Language Development; Memory;
Perception; Social Psychology*

Comparative Psychology

On a recent television talk show two men engaged in a brawl and had to be separated by the security staff. One of the men objected to the fact that the other had expressed an interest in having a relationship with his girlfriend. It is not uncommon, especially on television chat shows or in films, to see two men fighting over their perceived right to have a relationship with a woman. Similar sex-related aggressive behaviour can be observed in many other species, for example, baboons, chimpanzees, and even sheep. It is the similarity between animal and human behaviour that forms the basis of comparative psychology. However, the crucial question facing comparative psychology is the extent to which it is possible to generalise from animal to human behaviour.

There are a number of different approaches within comparative psychology which, to a certain extent, reflect different traditions of academic thought. In the United States the behaviourist tradition drew heavily on laboratory studies of animals such as pigeons and rats. One of the aims here was to identify the precise conditions under which learning takes place. In Europe, comparative psychology has its roots in the work of ethologists such as Konrad Lorenz, famous for his work on imprinting in young birds. An ethological approach focuses on studying animals in their natural environment rather than in a laboratory.

Another approach has relied on similarities between certain features in the human brain and animal brains. Although the human brain has unique and distinctive features, for example the neocortex, there are also structures that are found in other animals. The structures found in the lower part of the brain, just above the spinal cord, are very similar to those found in a wide range of other mammals. Unfortunately, this neurological approach often uses a method that involves surgically damaging specific parts of an animal's brain and studying the effects.

see also...

Behaviourism; Brain Structure; Conditioning; Ethics

Conditioning

Julian and his daughter Anna were at the cinema. Julian had bought a bag containing lots of different candy sweets. He offered the bag to Anna who sorted through it carefully until she found the blue one which she then proceeded to eat. One explanation for Anna's behaviour is that as a result of her previous experiences she had associated the blue-coloured candy with a pleasant taste.

Psychologists have always been interested in trying to understand how people learn. The behaviourist approach assumes that learning is based either on the association between two stimuli in the environment (classical conditioning) or on the association between a behaviour and its consequences (operant conditioning). It was a Russian scientist called Ivan Pavlov who first carried out a systematic study into the type of learning that is now referred to as classical conditioning. Pavlov was working in the early part of the twentieth century investigating the digestive system of dogs. As part of his work he used the fact that many animals, including dogs, salivate when food is placed in their mouths. However, during his work Pavlov made the interesting observation that any stimulus present in the environment immediately prior to the dogs being fed, such as a bell to signal feeding time or the dogs' food trays, could also be used to make the dogs salivate. The explanation is in terms of the dogs associating the environmental stimuli with food, where eventually the mere presence of the bell or tray will be sufficient to make the dogs salivate. In other words, the dogs have become conditioned to respond to the environmental stimuli.

Rewards are used widely in everyday life as a means of persuading people to behave in particular ways. Burrhus F. Skinner's operant conditioning assumes that behaviour is controlled by its consequences. Positive reinforcement increases the likelihood of the behaviour occurring again.

see also...

Behaviour Modification; Behaviour Therapy; Behaviourism; Skinner, Burrhus F.

Consciousness

onnie was playing football and got a bang on the head. The next thing he was aware of was waking up and hearing someone saying, 'Don't worry he's conscious again.' But what does it mean to be conscious? An influential view, proposed by William James at the turn of the twentieth century, suggests that consciousness is the constantly changing stream of awareness of internal and external events that we experience during our normal waking hours. Consciousness means us being aware of thoughts, feelings and perceptions.

It has been suggested that consciousness functions to monitor our self and the environment and also provides a means of controlling thought and behaviour. Our awareness constantly fluctuates between focusing on the external and internal worlds and, as anyone who has performed a mundane boring task will be aware, daydreaming is very much a part of our normal waking consciousness. Some daydreams are concerned with planning future events and actions whereas others are pure fantasy!

Freud made a distinction between two types of subconscious processes. Preconscious thoughts and processes can be brought into awareness by paying attention to them, whereas unconscious thoughts and processes are more or less permanently unavailable to consciousness. This distinction led to research which looked at the effects of images presented subliminally, that is, too quickly for people to be consciously aware of them. The findings suggest that subliminal images can indeed influence a person's mood and thought. For example, subliminal presentation of a happy or sad face affects the extent to which people like subsequent pictures. There have been some attempts to use subliminal messages in advertising campaigns, but the effects of subliminally presented information are not very strong and are unlikely to be influential in determining consumer behaviour.

see also...

Dreams; Freud, Sigmund; James, William; Repression; Sleep

Coping Strategies

Mr Munro had just started teaching and was finding one particular class very difficult. They just wouldn't cooperate and settle down to the work he gave them. Mr Munro was exhibiting many signs of stress, such as having difficulty concentrating, loss of appetite and feeling anxious when he thought about going to work. How can Mr Munro cope with his situation?

Psychologists make a distinction between two basic types of coping strategy – problem-focused strategies and emotion-focused strategies. Problem-focused strategies attempt to deal with those aspects of the environment that are responsible for the stress being experienced. So in Mr Munro's situation, problem-focused strategies would include seeking advice and assistance from his more experienced colleagues, planning alternative ways of delivering the lessons and motivating the class. In other words, he would engage in activities which were aimed at dealing directly with the stressful situation.

Emotion-focused strategies attempt to change the way a person thinks about a stressful situation. In this case, Mr Munro could tell himself that the behaviour of the class wasn't really that bad and that teenagers always test out new teachers. This would be an example of an emotion-focused strategy. Mr Munro would try to deal with the emotional consequences of the stress rather than attempt to change the situation. But does it make any difference which strategy Mr Munro uses?

There is evidence to suggest that in many situations an active problem-focused approach is more effective at reducing levels of stress than adopting an emotion-focused approach. Social support, in the form of friends and relatives and people in whom you can confide, is an important resource for coping with stress. However, the relationship between stress and social support is neither simple nor straightforward. For example, if a person under stress responds by becoming angry and aggressive it can undermine social support networks.

see also...

Anxiety; Health Psychology; Stress

Correlation

Andrea has just got home from a hard day at the office. She decides she needs to wind down before having something to eat, so she grabs a bottle of wine and a glass and settles down to play her favourite computer game, killing alien invaders. After a couple of hours and several glasses of wine Andrea checks her scores and notices that the more wine she drank the lower her scores became. This is not unexpected since there is plenty of evidence to suggest that alcohol has a detrimental effect on the performance of activities involving hand-eye coordination. Craig smokes about 15 cigarettes on a normal day, but if he is under a lot of pressure at work the number of cigarettes he smokes increases, whereas if things are going really well he smokes a lot less. Correlation is a statistical technique used to measure the relationship between two variables.

Correlations can be either negative or positive. A negative correlation means that the higher a person measures on one variable the lower they will measure on the other. The relationship between Andrea's performance and alcohol consumption is an example of a negative correlation. In other words, as her alcohol intake increases her scores go down. A positive correlation means that the higher a person measures on one variable the higher they will measure on the other, and vice-versa. So for Craig, there is a positive correlation between levels of stress and number of cigarettes he smokes. The higher the levels of stress the greater the number of cigarettes smoked and the lower the levels of stress the fewer cigarettes smoked.

An important fact to bear in mind when using correlations is that a relationship between two variables doesn't necessarily imply that one is causing the other to change. In Andrea's case, although her scores went down as she consumed more alcohol, there might be some other factor influencing her performance, for example, fatigue.

see also...

Experimental Method; Quantitative and Qualitative; Reliability and Validity; Survey

Defence Mechanisms

For several weeks Simon had been aware that a mole on the upper part of his arm was changing colour and seemed to be getting bigger. He convinced himself that there was nothing to worry about and he wasn't going to waste time by going to get it checked out at the health centre. According to Freud's psychodynamic theory, unconscious mental processes operate to protect people from unpleasant thoughts and emotions. These processes are called defence mechanisms. In Simon's case the mechanism in operation is denial, where he is refusing to acknowledge the reality that the changes to his mole could be cancerous. Simon's denial, and his subsequent failure to seek medical assistance, could be potentially life threatening. Other defence mechanisms include repression, projection and displacement.

Repression is the process that prevents thoughts that are extremely anxiety provoking from gaining access to our conscious awareness. Freud saw repression as the most important defence mechanism. Mike is a very hostile person but when confronted about it he refuses to accept that he is hostile and argues that the problem is really to do with other people being hostile towards him. This is an example of projection, where Mike is attributing his undesirable characteristics to other people. Jenny had been working on a report for a couple of weeks and when she gave it to her manager she felt it was a pretty good piece of work. Her manager didn't even say, 'Thanks', which made Jenny feel somewhat annoyed. When she got home Jenny shouted at her husband and the kids for fairly trivial things. Her anger was being displaced from work to home where she was letting it out in a less threatening situation.

People use defence mechanisms in very flexible and creative ways and it is not possible to predict which defence mechanism will be used by a particular person in a specific situation.

see also...

False Memories; Freud, Sigmund; Jung, Carl; Psychodynamic Approaches; Repression

Dementia

Derek was playing a round of golf with three of his friends. He was the first to the tee and hit his ball straight down the middle of the fairway. The other three members of the foursome played their first shots and then Derek put down another ball on a tee. His friends reminded him that he had already played his first shot. This happened a further five times as they played their round of golf. Throughout the round, as he was waiting for the others to play their shots, Derek invariably forgot where he had hit his ball. Derek is suffering from Alzheimer's disease which is one of the most common forms of dementia.

Dementia is a general term which refers to a progressive deterioration in a person's intellectual, emotional and motor functioning. Alzheimer's disease accounts for approximately half of all cases of dementia. Other causes of dementia include multi-infarct dementia which results from a series of small strokes (or infarcts) which destroy various parts of the brain. People suffering from AIDS are also at risk of developing dementia since in some cases the virus can directly attack the brain.

It is still not clear exactly what causes Alzheimer's disease, and it could be that there are different forms of the disease with different causes. There is some evidence that it seems to run in families, suggesting that it has a genetic basis. Further evidence for the role of genetics comes from studies of people with Down's syndrome (a genetic disorder), many of whom develop symptoms similar to Alzheimer's disease in late middle age. However, some people with no family history also develop the condition. It has been suggested that in some cases Alzheimer's disease can be the result of head injury. For example, some boxers show brain damage similar to that of Alzheimer's patients. Diagnosing Alzheimer's disease is very difficult when the patient is alive, since the symptoms are similar to many other forms of dementia. It is only through an examination of a patient's brain during an autopsy that a definitive diagnosis can be made.

see also...

Ageing; Brain Structure; Biopsychology; Clinical Psychology; Neurons

Depression

Gareth's friends have noticed a change in him during the last couple of weeks. He doesn't seem to be interested in any of the things he normally enjoys and he has been taking time off work. Whenever his friends ask him if he wants to go out or go to a football game his response is, 'I can't be bothered'. At other times he appears to be either very irritable or to have difficulty concentrating. Gareth's physical appearance has also changed, he has lost a lot of weight. Two weeks later Gareth takes an overdose of sleeping pills. Gareth has been exhibiting the signs of clinical depression.

Approximately six per cent of the population will be suffering from depression at any one time. Depression refers to a pattern of symptoms that include mood changes, loss of interest in any activity, feelings of worthlessness, loss of energy, eating disorders and suicidal thoughts and behaviour. However, the experience of depression can vary considerably from one person to another and it has been suggested that there are a number of different forms of depression.

A distinction has been made between depression that occurs in response to some life event and depression that doesn't appear to be linked to an external cause. One form of depression is referred to as 'major depressive disorder'. A major feature of this form of depression is a loss of interest in all the activities the person usually enjoys. Major depressive disorder is an extremely severe form of depression, but can be relatively short-lived. In bipolar depression, or manic depression, periods of elation, often accompanied by grandiose ideas, alternate with the periods of depression.

Two chemicals (serotonin and norepinephrine) found in the brain appear to be implicated in some forms of depression. Antidepressants work by altering the activity of these two chemicals. Other methods of treating depression include cognitive-behavioural therapy.

see also...

Anxiety; Clinical Psychology; Cognitive-Behavioural Therapy; Neurotransmitters; Schizophrenia

Developmental Psychology

Jayne watched her two children, Joshua aged ten and Amelia aged nine, playing in the park. It was a beautiful autumn day. Joshua was playing on the swings on his own. Amelia had met a friend from school and was talking to her about their favourite pop group. Joshua jumped off the swing, grabbed a handful of leaves and threw them at Amelia and her friend for no apparent reason. Jayne wondered why Joshua behaved like this and what she should do about it. At school he continually got into trouble for pushing other pupils and being too aggressive in the classroom. Amelia, on the other hand, was never in trouble at school, had lots of friends and was comfortable in most social situations. Lots of questions were racing through Jayne's mind. Was Joshua's behaviour inherited? Was it something to do with the way Jayne had brought him up? Why were Joshua and Amelia so different? The questions confronting Jayne are typical of those faced by many parents and there are no easy answers to them!

Developmental psychology is the study of how and why people grow and change throughout their lives.

One question that has attracted considerable attention within developmental psychology is: How does our environment interact with our genetic make-up to influence development? This is often referred to as the 'nature versus nurture' controversy. If we consider Joshua and Amelia it is difficult to say whether the outcome is the product of biology or the environment. Joshua may well have a biological predisposition to behave aggressively whereas Amelia may be biologically predisposed to be sociable and placid. On the other hand, Joshua's behaviour could be a consequence of the fact that when Joshua behaves badly his father responds inconsistently, either with physical punishment or by just ignoring it, whereas Amelia never receives any form of physical punishment. So it is very difficult in cases like this to determine whether the outcome is the result of biology or the environment.

see also...

Adolescence; Cognitive Development; Cognitive Psychology; Language Development; Social Development; Social Psychology

Dreams

Dreams are a common feature of everyday life but their function and operation are still not fully understood. Freud argued that all mental events, including dreams, have a meaning. He suggested that all our dreams reflect some underlying unconscious desire. Freud made a distinction between the actual content of the dream and its underlying meaning, which he referred to as its latent content. According to Freud it is possible to uncover the latent content of a dream by the use of a technique called free-association. In free-association the person says the first thing that comes to mind when presented with different parts of the dream.

It was once thought that dreaming was associated with one particular stage of sleep referred to as 'rapid eye movement' (REM) sleep. When people are woken from REM sleep they are able to report an ongoing dream in about 80 per cent of cases. However, dreaming has also been found to take place in other stages of sleep. Nevertheless the relationship between REM sleep and dreaming has provided a technique for investigating dreams. If you have to rely on people recording their dreams when they wake naturally, it is a very time-consuming process, since people typically report only two or three dreams each week. By bringing people into a laboratory and waking them up when they are in REM sleep, it is possible to collect several dream reports in a single night. There is evidence from a variety of sources that events and anxieties from a person's waking life can have an influence on the content of his or her dreams. For example, one study gave people a list of phrases to study before going to sleep and it was found that the content of the phrases was reflected in their dreams. However, in many cases the content of the phrases had been considerably distorted. For example one phrase, 'the sword is pulled from the stone' resulted in a dream in which the person was trying to pull a cork out of a bottle. A biological account proposes that dreams are the result of the brain interpreting the spontaneous activity that occurs in various parts of our brain during sleep.

see also...

Biopsychology; Cognitive Psychology; Freud, Sigmund; Sleep

Dyslexia

Julian started school shortly after his fifth birthday. Up until that point his parents saw Julian as a happy, outgoing child. However, soon after starting school he became withdrawn and difficult. Julian's teacher suspected he had a learning disability and arranged for him to be assessed by a psychologist. Julian scored above average on most of the tests given to him by the psychologist, but well below average on word and letter recognition tests. It turned out that Julian's specific problem was dyslexia.

Dyslexia is defined in a number of different ways, but broadly speaking it is a problem with reading. There are two main types of dyslexia: developmental dyslexia, the type exhibited by Julian, and acquired dyslexia. Developmental dyslexia usually becomes apparent during childhood when the child is learning to read. Typical problems include translating printed words into spoken words, letter reversal, for example reading 'd' for 'b', mispronunciation, and understanding spoken language. Recent estimates suggest that somewhere in the region of ten to 15 per cent of children have some degree of developmental dyslexia.

The causes of developmental dyslexia are not clear. There is some evidence that dyslexia is inherited and it is not uncommon to find several members of a family with varying levels of dyslexia. One line of research suggests that the problems experienced by developmental dyslexics are the result of a problem with phonological processing. Phonological processing refers to the conversion of sounds into words and words into sounds. In order to read simple words aloud, for example 'dog', the printed letters on the page must be converted into a sequence of spoken sounds. These sounds must then be put together in the correct order to produce the word. It appears that it is these activities that are problematic for people with developmental dyslexia.

Acquired dyslexia refers to the forms of dyslexia that are the result of a brain injury.

see also...

Language Development; Non-Verbal Communication; Psychological Tests

Eating Disorders

Just as physical health can affect eating, so too can psychological factors. Eating disorders are symptoms of underlying emotional and psychological disorders and are not really about food. Food and eating are simply the means by which people express their difficulties. Most eating disorders develop between the ages of 15 and 25 years, although in some cases they can develop in children as young as seven or eight. Two of the most common eating disorders are anorexia nervosa and bulimia nervosa, commonly referred to as anorexia and bulimia. Both are associated with low levels of psychological well-being and a variety of physical health problems.

Anorexia affects many more women than men, with fewer than ten per cent of anorexic cases being men. The symptoms of anorexia include a marked weight loss and a refusal to maintain body weight, along with a morbid fear of weight gain and a distorted body image. Bulimia is characterized by episodes of bingeing which are usually followed by some method of getting rid of the food such as self-induced vomiting. The causes of eating disorders vary from one person to another. It likely that in each case there will be a combination of personal, social and cultural factors responsible for the problems.

People who develop anorexia are likely to have shown high levels of conformity when they were children and also have a high level of control over their emotions. People with bulimia are likely to be good students or employees and present a self-assured image in public. However, they usually have a low self-esteem and are unhappy and depressed when not in the presence of other people. One of the major differences between anorexia and bulimia is that people with bulimia often recognize that they do have an eating disorder, whereas anorexics don't. In combination with other approaches, psychotherapy appears to be effective in helping people with anorexia and bulimia.

see also...

Clinical Psychology; Cognitive-Behavioural Therapy; Depression; Psychotherapy

Emotions

Mary was talking to Jessica about her day at work. 'You wouldn't believe what happened today at work,' Mary said in a rather indignant manner. 'I needed to staple a lot of papers together and I always keep my stapler in my left-hand drawer. So I opened the drawer and it had gone! I spent the next half-hour looking everywhere for it. Then along strolls the guy who has the desk next to mine and, cool as you like, just puts the stapler on my desk and says, "Thanks, mine's broke". I couldn't believe it. I was so angry I just wanted to go and grab him and tell him he should ask before he takes other people's things. I was that angry I was shaking.' Mary is expressing her anger about the behaviour of her colleague.

Emotions can be thought of as comprising three components, a feeling, a physiological change and a state of readiness for action. In Mary's case there was her feeling of anger towards her colleague, a bodily change that results in Mary physically shaking and, finally, there was a state of readiness for action in that she wanted to go and grab hold of her colleague.

So what purpose do emotions serve? It has been argued that emotions have developed in order to help us deal with an environment that is rapidly changing. Anger and fear are an indication that things are not going according to plan, whereas an emotion such as happiness signals that we are achieving our goals. It has been suggested that there are six basic emotions common to all cultures and languages: happiness, surprise, fear, sadness, anger and disgust. One line of research into emotions has focused on the development of emotional responses in infants. It would appear that by the age of ten to 12 months infants have the ability to express differentially the emotions of happiness and distress. At this age they can also recognize major changes of emotional behaviour in their primary caregivers, such as when their caregiver is happy or angry, but just how subtle the distinctions they are able to make at this age is unclear.

see also...

Biopsychology; Coping Strategies; Health Psychology; Stress

Episodic, Semantic and Procedural Memory

Norman was sitting in the garden enjoying a well-earned glass of lemonade. He had just dug over the vegetable plot and while he relaxed his mind began to wander. First, he started thinking about his wedding day all those years ago. He remembered walking down the aisle as if it was yesterday. Then he started to think about all the facts he had learned at school: Paris is the capital of France, Everest is the highest mountain in the world – so much information! Just then, Norman heard someone shouting and looked up to see his grandson riding towards him on his new bicycle.

If we consider Norman's experience in the garden it also becomes clear that we can identify different kinds of information in our long-term memory. Psychologists have suggested that these different types of information are located in different stores in our long-term memory. We have countless memories of our own personal experiences that are associated with a particular time and place – just like Norman's vivid memories of his wedding day. This type of memory is referred to as episodic memory.

Semantic memory, on the other hand, is our knowledge of the world and the language we use to describe it. We can usually retrieve information from our semantic memory very rapidly, for example, most people could tell us which was the highest mountain in the world within a couple of seconds. This suggests that information in our semantic memories is highly organized. Our episodic memories and semantic memories can be described in words with relative ease. However, this isn't the case for all the information in our long-term memory. For example, try describing to someone else how you maintain your balance on a bicycle. Procedural memory is our memory relating to things such as riding a bicycle or playing the piano. Once we have learned to ride a bicycle or play the piano we don't normally forget, but it is impossible to translate that kind of knowledge into language.

see also...

Eyewitness Testimony; False Memories; Forgetting; Memory; Primacy and Recency Effects; Schemas and Scripts

Ethics

Stanley Milgram carried out a series of experiments in the 1960s. The participants were told they were taking part in an experiment to investigate the relationship between punishment and learning. Participants were then instructed to punish the 'learner' in the next room whenever they made a mistake using, what they believed to be, an electric shock generator. The switches were labelled from 15 volts (slight shock) to 450 volts (danger: severe shock). Participants were instructed to start by administering a slight shock and then increase the voltage every time the learner made an error. In fact, the learner was a confederate of the experimenter and didn't actually receive any electric shocks, but just behaved as if he were by protesting and eventually screaming as the voltage of the supposed shocks increased.

Milgram wasn't studying learning at all. Rather he was interested in the extent to which people would obey instructions. His studies raise a number of ethical issues for the way in which psychologists conduct research programmes. First, the participants were deceived, not only about the true nature of the experiment but they were also led to believe that they were subjecting an innocent person to electric shocks. Many psychology experiments involve some degree of deception. In such cases the psychologist should ensure that the participants are provided with sufficient details about the study and also reduce any distress that may have been caused by the experiment. Second, it is important in any research that the participants have the right to withdraw at any time. Third, participants should be able to give their voluntary informed consent to take part in the study.

The overriding concern of psychologists carrying out research should be to ensure that their participants are protected against any psychological or physical harm. Professional bodies that regulate the conduct of psychologists publish guidelines that govern the treatment of research participants.

see also...

Experimental Method; Quantitative and Qualitative; Reliability and Validity; Social Psychology

Experimental Method

Jan and Anna are students studying for their end of course exam. Jan remembers reading somewhere that the best way to remember something is to make sure that you really understand it and make links between the information you are trying to learn and your existing knowledge (learning by understanding). Anna, on the other hand, believes that the best way to remember information is to read it over and over again until you can remember it (learning by rote). We could set up an experiment to find out who is correct.

Most experiments start with a prediction about what will happen – this is referred to as a hypothesis. Jan and Anna's hypothesis could be something like, 'Learning by rote and learning by understanding will produce different levels of recall in a subsequent test.' In experiments, the effect that manipulating some aspect of a situation has on participants' behaviour is observed. In Anna and Jan's case the variable being manipulated is the learning method and the behaviour being observed is their performance on a test. In order to test out the hypothesis a basic experimental design would involve Anna and Jan learning some information using their different methods and then being tested to see how much they could remember.

One of the main aims of an experiment is to establish a causal relationship between variables, so that when the experiment is complete we are able to say with some confidence that the variable we are manipulating is actually responsible for the behaviour we are observing. This means that we have to be sure that there are not any other variables that could be responsible for participants' behaviour. In the case above, there are a number of factors that we would need to control when setting up the experiment. For example, we would need to ensure that Anna and Jan learned the material at the same time of day and that they had exactly the same amount of time to learn and recall the information.

see also...

Correlation; Ethics; Probability; Quantitative and Qualitative; Reliability and Validity; Survey

Eyewitness Testimony

The statement, 'I saw it with my own eyes' is often used as a way of enhancing the credibility of a person's account of a particular event. In many criminal cases the prosecution case relies on the accounts of eyewitnesses, but can we rely on the accuracy of a testimony given by an eyewitness? This is an important question since many juries place considerable trust in the evidence given by eyewitnesses.

Psychologists have established that under certain conditions it is remarkably easy for the memory of an eyewitness to become distorted. Experiments have devised a number of experiments to investigate factors influencing the accuracy of eyewitness accounts. In a typical experiment participants are shown a short film depicting a particular incident such as a car accident. The experimenter then asks the participants specific questions about the incident. One series of studies, carried out by Elizabeth Loftus and her colleagues, investigated the effect of seemingly minor changes in the wording of the questions. For example, after watching a depiction of a car crash, one group of participants was asked, 'About how fast were the cars going when they *hit* each other?' The other group was asked, 'About how fast were the cars going when they *smashed into* each other?' The relatively minor change of replacing 'hit' with 'smashed into' had a significant impact on the accounts given by the two groups. When the verb 'smashed' was used, participants' estimates of the speed of the cars were higher than when the verb 'hit' was used. Also participants were more likely to report seeing broken glass even though there was no broken glass present.

Eyewitness accounts can also be distorted in other ways. For example, an individual's expectations about what is likely to happen in specific situations can often have as much influence on what is remembered as what actually took place. These findings have important implications for the legal system.

see also...

Episodic, Semantic and Procedural Memory; False Memories; Forgetting; Memory; Primacy and Recency Effects

Eysenck, Hans J.

Hans J. Eysenck was born in Germany in 1916 and died in London in 1997. Soon after his birth his parents separated and eventually divorced. Eysenck was brought up in Berlin by his maternal grandmother who died in a Nazi concentration camp. He was a natural athlete, and as well as becoming German Junior Tennis Champion he was also a good amateur boxer. Eysenck moved to London in 1934 and was awarded a PhD by the University of London in 1940.

Eysenck was a longstanding critic of psychotherapy and advocated behaviour therapy as an alternative. He is perhaps best known for his contributions to personality theory. Eysenck proposed that personality consists of a number of traits. According to this view the traits that go to make up a person's personality give rise to tendencies to behave in particular ways. For example, the fact that Nancy is talkative, smiles and participates in social events could reflect a personality trait such as 'sociability'. Whereas Bill's behaviour of frequent scowling, angry outbursts and avoiding social events could reflect a personality trait of 'angry hostility'.

Eysenck identified three major personality traits (sometimes referred to as types) which he labelled: extraversion, neuroticism and psychotism. He developed a questionnaire (the Eysenck Personality Questionnaire) aimed at measuring the extent to which people were extravert, neurotic and psychotic. People scoring highly on the extravert scale will tend to be sociable, outgoing and willing to take risks, whereas those scoring a low mark (introverts) will tend to be cautious, withdrawn and serious. People scoring highly on the neuroticism scale will tend to be anxious, moody and have low self-esteem. High scores on the psychoticism scale reflect a tendency to be aggressive, impulsive and anti-social, whereas low scores reflect a tendency to control one's impulses and be empathic.

Eysenck believed that heredity has a large part to play in determining differences in personality.

see also...

Behaviour Therapy; Freud, Sigmund; Jung, Carl; Personality; Psychodynamic Approaches

False Memories

Sigmund Freud's concept of repression plays a central role in the debate surrounding false memories. Freud suggested that memories for unpleasant events could be repressed and become unavailable to our conscious awareness. The false memory debate has arisen from the occurrence of recovered memories – where adults report remembering specific childhood events, after experiencing many years of not being aware that the events actually took place.

Some psychotherapists believe that certain mental and physical problems occurring in adult life are the result of childhood sexual abuse. These therapists believe that memories of sexual abuse are repressed, making them unavailable for recollection under normal circumstances. So at the time of the initial consultation with the psychotherapist, the patient will have some emotional problem but is not aware that he or she may have been abused as a child. A controversial technique called Recovered Memory Therapy is used which aims to enable patients to recover the memories of abuse into consciousness. A common outcome of Recovered Memory Therapy is that patients believe that they were sexually abused as a child. Such an outcome has legal as well as emotional implications for the patient and their family.

It is important to make a distinction between false memories – where an event never really happened, and incorrect memories – where an event occurred, but some of the details are not recalled accurately. Elizabeth Loftus has demonstrated that it is possible to generate false memories in adults. In one study a teenage boy became completely convinced that at the age of two he had got lost in a shopping mall and a stranger had found him and reunited him with his parents. This event had never happened. On the other hand, incidents of child abuse occur all too frequently and it is likely that in some cases memories of the abuse are repressed.

see also...

Episodic, Semantic and Procedural Memory; Eyewitness Testimony; Forgetting; Memory; Repression

Forensic Psychology

Forensic psychology is concerned with applying psychological knowledge to the criminal justice system. Forensic psychologists provide advice to legislators, judges, police officers and lawyers and can play a role in criminal investigations. One technique used by forensic psychologists to assist the police is offender profiling. This is where the forensic psychologist uses information from previous crimes to build up a profile of the person likely to have committed them. Offender profiling has received considerable attention in the media and may appear to be exciting, but very few psychologists get the opportunity to be involved in this type of work.

Psychologists have also developed specific techniques for interviewing witnesses and suspects. For example, the Cognitive Interview has been developed to help witnesses of crimes recall as much information as possible about the event. The interview follows a set sequence and requires the witness to think about the event in different ways. For example, one part of the interview asks the witness to report the incident in reverse order. Each strategy in the interview is designed to help the witness construct a new description of the event which increases the likelihood of more information being recalled correctly. The cognitive interview reliably increases the amount of information elicited from witnesses. Forensic psychologists also make a contribution within the court system, for example, in assessing the offender's mental state at the time of the offence. In the United States, they are often asked to evaluate the extent to which potential jury members may be prejudicial for or against the case.

Most forensic psychologists work in prisons or high security psychiatric hospitals. One of their major roles within these institutions is to provide a range of therapies and treatment programmes.

see also...

Clinical Psychology; Health Psychology; Sport Psychology; Work and Organizational Psychology

Forgetting

Ryan is in the dining room lifting up cushions, looking behind the ornaments. He has forgotten where he left his car keys for the third time this week! Tracy goes to the cinema at least once a week and she is telling her friend about a film she watched last week, but she can't remember the name of one of the actors. Janice has just changed her mobile phone and is having trouble remembering the new number. No matter how hard she tries whenever someone asks for her telephone number she always starts by giving her old number. Most of us can remember what we did yesterday, but how many people can remember exactly what they were doing on 7 October 1998? Unless that date has some specific significance, most people will have no idea what they were doing on that day. Sometimes we just forget some of the details about an event, while at other times we forget things altogether. So why do we forget?

One theory of forgetting – decay theory – suggests that memories simply fade away as they get older. Another theory suggests that forgetting occurs because new learning disrupts or interferes with existing memories and vice-versa. This is referred to as the interference theory of forgetting. The problems Janice is encountering in remembering her new telephone number could be explained using interference theory. Previously stored telephone numbers could be interfering with the retrieval of her new number. In everyday life interference is most likely to occur if the new information is similar to our existing memories. This could account for Tracy's inability to recall the name of the actor. Because she watches a lot of films, Tracy's long-term memory contains the names of many actors, so there is a possibility that these existing memories can interfere with her ability to remember the actor's name. It is important to bear in mind that just because we cannot remember something at one moment in time doesn't necessarily mean that the information has been permanently lost.

see also...

Episodic, Semantic and Procedural Memory; Eyewitness Testimony; False Memories; Memory

Freud, Sigmund

Sigmund Freud was born on 6 May 1856 in what is now Pribor in the Czech Republic. He died in Hampstead, London, on 23 September 1939. He spent most of his life in Vienna after graduating as a Doctor of Medicine from the University of Vienna. In 1900 he published one of his major works, *The Interpretation of Dreams* in which he argued that repressed sexual desires manifest themselves in a disguised form in dreams. In 1902 he was appointed to a professorship in Vienna where he continued to develop his ideas and a circle of like-minded associates that resulted in the formation, in 1908, of the Vienna Psycho-Analytical Society.

The effect that Sigmund Freud had on the development of psychology cannot be underestimated. He was the originator of psychoanalysis, a term he first used in a paper published in 1891. Freud used the term psychoanalysis to refer to a theory of personality and also a therapeutic approach to treating psychological disorders. Freud's theory is referred to as a psychodynamic approach because it emphasizes the dynamic and conflicting nature of mental processes. Psychodynamic theories have two fundamental ideas. First, people are often not aware of their motives for behaving in a particular way, in other words, their motives are unconscious. Second, processes called defence mechanisms operate to protect the mind from unpleasant or anxiety provoking thoughts and feelings.

Freud suggested that at any moment in time we are aware only of some of our thoughts – our conscious thoughts. Other thoughts are either preconscious and can be brought into awareness without much difficulty, or are unconscious. According to Freud it is very difficult, or sometimes impossible, to become aware of our unconscious thoughts. Unpleasant and traumatic events are often located in the unconscious. Freud believed that psychological problems, such as anxiety disorders, are the result of conflicts between a person's unconscious thoughts.

see also...

Defence Mechanisms; Jung, Carl; Personality; Psychodynamic Approaches; Repression

Gender Development

Rebecca, who is seven years old, and James, who is three, are playing at dressing up. James is wearing a pair of his mother's shoes and an old dress and Rebecca is trying on some of her mother's old lipstick. They are joined by their sister, Mary, who is five years old. They tell her that she can join in and play as well. James says he is going to be a mummy when he grows up. Rebecca tells him not to be so silly. 'You're a boy,' she says, 'and you're always going to be a boy.' Mary says, 'He can be a mummy if he wants to be. He's just got to wear the right clothes.' Children's language and mental abilities become increasingly complex as they get older. Not only does their understanding of the social world develop but also their understanding of what it means to be male or female.

Rebecca, James and Mary all have different understandings about what it means to be male or female. Several theories have attempted to account for how children develop a sense of gender identity. Lawrence Kohlberg proposed that children go through three stages in the development of a gender identity. In the first stage, when children are between two and five years of age, they develop the ability to identify themselves and other children as either male or female. A key feature of the second stage (at age five or six years) is that children become aware that their gender will remain the same as they get older. However, children at this age are sometimes less clear that this applies also to other people. For example, some children believe that if girls behave and dress like boys they can become boys. In the final stage, children realize that a person's gender cannot be changed by superficial factors such as wearing someone else's clothes. An alternative account proposed by Albert Bandura and Walter Mischel suggests that children acquire knowledge about gender roles through observational learning, in other words, by observing other people who act as role models.

see also...

Developmental Psychology; Gender and Sex; Social Development; Stereotypes

Gender and Sex

Shirley had spent the day visiting her sister and her two young nephews. As she relaxed with her husband later that evening, Shirley began to tell him about their nephews. She said, 'You know, they are on the go all the time. They can't sit still for two minutes; all they want to do is play ball. Typical boys.' Shirley has a set of expectations and beliefs about what constitutes appropriate behaviour for boys and girls. These beliefs and expectations are referred to as sex role stereotypes (or gender role stereotypes). Is there any evidence that stereotypes such as Shirley's are grounded in real differences between the abilities of boys and girls?

The findings of studies that have investigated sex differences in ability suggest that there are considerably more similarities than there are differences. Despite the fact that the differences between the sexes are very small, it is still the case that in many societies there is a tendency to encourage the development of different behaviours in boys and girls. For example, girls are encouraged to be supportive and sensitive, whereas boys are encouraged to be assertive and competitive; men are expected to be dominant and women submissive. However, there is evidence that some countries, typically technologically developed, individualistic, urban societies, are becoming more egalitarian. In psychology a distinction is made between the terms sex and gender. The terms sex and sexual identity refer to a person's biological status as either male or female. A person's gender and gender identity refer to the sense and awareness of being either male or female. A person's gender develops in the social and cultural setting of their early childhood, whereas their sex is determined at birth. In most cases a person's gender corresponds to their sex, but not for everyone. For example, transsexuals feel they have been born into a body of the opposite sex, so there is a disparity between their biological sexual identity and their gender identity. It has been argued that children begin to acquire their gender identities at two or three years of age.

see also...

Developmental Psychology;
Gender Development; Stereotypes

Gestalt Psychology

Caroline is seated in her favourite armchair with a glass of sherry in one hand and a mince pie in the other. She is looking at the lights on the Christmas tree which give the impression of a point of light racing around the tree. Most of us have had the experience of watching lights that give the impression of motion. In reality the motion is an illusion created by the bulbs going on and off in a particular order. Although the individual bulbs are stationary, working together the whole effect is one of movement.

Gestalt psychology was developed in Germany in the early part of the twentieth century with the central belief that the whole is greater than the sum of its parts. Gestalt is a German word which means 'form' or 'whole'. The development of gestalt psychology was in part a reaction against the structuralist approach which attempted to analyze experiences by breaking them down into smaller units. German psychologist Max Wertheimer was a key figure in the promotion of gestalt psychology and is credited with founding it. He argued that it is a mistake to try to understand human behaviour by breaking it down into small pieces or elements. Gestalt psychology provided a set of principles to describe how perceptions are organized into meaningful wholes. One of these proposes that we group together items that are physically close to each other. For example, we would perceive (I I I I I I) as three pairs. Whereas, (I I I I I I) would be more likely to be perceived as six individual items.

Gestalt psychology has also given rise to a type of therapy. Gestalt therapy assumes that a person's awareness can become disjointed and incomplete. It focuses on a person's immediate experiences and the therapist attempts to help the individual fill in any gaps. It is argued that we often are reluctant to express our feelings and this creates the gaps. In Gestalt therapy clients are encouraged to express their feelings in the 'here and now' rather than to discuss why they have particular feelings.

see also...

Humanistic Psychology; Kohler, Wolfgang; Perception; Problem Solving; Psychotherapy

Groups

We are all members of at least one group, for example, a family group, an ethnic group or a work group, and most of us move in and out of numerous groups throughout our lives. Groups consist of a set of individuals who influence each other and can vary along a number of dimensions. For example, some groups are small whereas others are large, some groups endure for many years while others last for only a couple of days, some groups are highly organized but others are much more informal. It has been suggested that belonging to a group satisfies basic psychological needs, such as a need to be with others. A group also provides its members with a sense of identity.

Groups develop informal rules, or norms, that guide the behaviour and the thoughts and attitudes of their members. Whether or not members of a group conform to its norms depends to a large extent on the members' view of the group. If membership of the group is important to a perso, he or she is likely to conform to its norms. When a group is working on a task its members often take on different roles. For example, some people take on a leadership role ensuring that the group completes its task, others may act to release tension by keeping people amused, and some may work to ensure that things run smoothly and there is minimal conflict within the group.

A study carried out by Philip Zimbardo provided a dramatic illustration of the extent to which people are capable of taking on specific roles. Students volunteered to play the roles of prisoners and guards in a simulated prison. The outcomes of the study were so extreme that it was terminated after only six days. The guards became increasingly aggressive and abusive and the prisoners became depressed and extremely anxious. Even though all the participants in the experiment were college students they readily took on the roles assigned to them and behaved in a way they believed was consistent with the role.

> ## see also...
> *Asch, Solomon; Social Facilitation; Social Psychology; Stereotypes*

Health Psychology

Leslie and Patrick are in their mid-fifties. Both of them are considerably overweight and don't do much physical exercise. Their fathers both died in their early sixties from a heart attack. After the millennium celebrations they make resolutions to lose weight and do more exercise. Over the next couple of months Leslie sticks to his resolution and loses 20 pounds, whereas Patrick doesn't change his lifestyle at all.

Health psychology is concerned with psychological factors involved in health and disease and in particular with why some people engage in healthy behaviours and others don't. One model that attempts to explain this is the health belief model. According to this model a person's beliefs about the extent to which they are susceptible to a specific health threat and their beliefs about the effectiveness of specific behaviours in reducing the risk are important factors in determining behaviour. So, the difference between Leslie's and Patrick's behaviour could be explained in the following way. Leslie believes that he is at risk from heart disease and also believes that the consequences could be very serious for himself and his family. He thinks that the proposed diet and exercise plan will be effective and not too difficult for him to stick to. Patrick, on the other hand, does not believe he is at risk, and thinks that diets and exercise are a waste of his very valuable time.

One of the major reasons for the growth of health psychology has been a shift in the causes of death in Western countries. At the beginning of the twentieth century diseases such as tuberculosis, diphtheria and influenza were major causes of death. At the beginning of the twenty-first century the major cause of death in European countries is heart disease. It has been suggested that unhealthy behaviour can account for as much as 50 per cent of current mortality rates. One of the aims of health psychology is to explore ways in which people can be supported in developing healthier lifestyles.

see also...

Anxiety; Biopsychology; Clinical Psychology; Coping Strategies; Stress

49

Humanistic Psychology

Humanistic psychology emerged as a clearly identifiable approach within psychology during the 1950s. One of the main concerns of humanistic psychology is to focus on people's capacity for self-awareness and conscious experience of themselves and the world they live in. This is in contrast to the approach taken by behaviourists who are not concerned with the reflexive nature of human thought but rather on behaviours that can be directly observed.

As you are reading this book you may decide to go and make a cup of coffee, or you may look out of the window and realize that it is such a wonderful day that you put on your shoes and go for walk. On the other hand you might choose to continue reading this page before you do anything else. These are examples where we are exercising our power of choice. In psychology the ability to make decisions and have control over what we do is referred to as personal agency. Humanistic psychology extends the notion of personal agency to include the idea that we can all play a role in determining the kind of person we are. It proposes that in order to understand people we need to focus on the whole person rather than studying specific aspects in isolation.

Carl Rogers developed an approach to therapy based on humanistic psychology called client-centred or person-centred therapy. One of the assumptions underlying the therapy is the belief that sometimes there is a difference between the way individuals sees themselves and the way they actually behave. For example, Fred thinks of himself as a calm, relaxed person, but in many situations he finds himself behaving in an aggressive manner. One of the aims of client-centred therapy is to reduce the gap between a person's current experiences and their ideal self. In contrast to Freud's psychodynamic therapy, which focuses on past experiences, humanistic therapy is more concerned with the present 'here and now' of a person's experience.

see also...

Behaviourism; Clinical Psychology; Gestalt Psychology; Freud, Sigmund; Psychotherapy

Impression Formation

At work Carol was introduced to a new colleague. Carol tried to engage her in a conversation but she seemed to be rather aloof. Although they had spoken only very briefly Carol had already decided that she didn't really like her new colleague and thought that she would have trouble coping with the job. Throughout our lives we meet numerous people and often we appear to make decisions very quickly about whether or not we like them. Impression formation is concerned with the factors that determine our reactions to people when we meet them for the first time.

In Carol's case it is clear that she knows very little about her new colleague and doesn't really have a great deal of information on which to base her judgement. When we are making judgements about others we appear to make an assumption that if a person has one characteristic or trait, they will also have other related traits. So Carol is using her own personal theory of personality that she has developed through her own experiences about what personality traits are likely to be found together. This theory is referred to as an implicit personality theory. In the majority of cases we make judgements about people on two dimensions. The first dimension relates to sociability and the extent to which we find people either sociable, helpful and warm or unsociable and cold. It seems that Carol has decided her colleague is towards the unsociable end of this dimension. The second dimension relates to intellectual capacity and the extent to which we judge a person to be stupid and foolish or skilful, persistent and intelligent. Carol has decided that her colleague is towards the stupid end of this dimension. As well as forming impressions on the basis of our judgements of a person's personality, we are also influenced by the physical appearance of the person. Research suggests that individuals who are rated as being physically attractive are also rated as being sociable, interesting and exciting.

see also...

Attitudes; Interpersonal Attraction; Intimate Relationships; Stereotypes

Intelligence

Beth was telling her sister about her new boyfriend. She said, 'He's tall, has dark hair and is really intelligent.' We all know what it means to be tall and have dark hair, but what does it mean to be intelligent? Defining intelligence is a problem that has confronted psychologists throughout the twentieth century. The term intelligence is used in different ways by different people and there is currently no definition that is universally accepted within psychology.

The British psychologist Charles Spearman proposed that intelligence is a general quality that underlies performance on all tasks. So if a person is good at one thing they will be good at everything. In contrast, the American psychologist, Louis L. Thurstone, argued that intelligence was better thought of as consisting of a number of different abilities that were more or less independent of each other. In other words a person could perform well on one task and relatively poorly on another. A more recent theory, along similar lines to Thurstone's, has been developed by Howard Gardner who argues that there are six distinct types of intelligence. The first three of these intelligences are mathematical intelligence, spatial intelligence and verbal intelligence. These are the abilities tested in many conventional intelligence tests. The other three intelligences proposed by Gardner are rather more controversial. They are musical intelligence, personal intelligence (the ability to understand your own and other people's emotions), and bodily-kinesthetic intelligence (the ability to perform skilled body movements or manipulate intricate objects, for example, in dancing and making jewelry).

Whether intelligence is best conceived of as a combination of separate abilities or a single quality is unresolved, but it is likely that the answer lies in a combination of the two views. Intelligence is conventionally measured using one of a range of different intelligence tests.

see also...

Intelligence Quotient; Personality; Psychological Tests; Qualitative and Quantitative; Reliability and Validity

Intelligence Quotient (IQ)

Natasha was picking up her son from school and she overheard two mothers talking. One said, 'Did you know Donald has an IQ of 120?' But what does it mean to have an IQ of 120?

Psychologists have developed a number of tests that aim to assess a person's intelligence relative to other people. One of the first tests was developed in France by Alfred Binet and Theodore Simon in the early part of the twentieth century. They were concerned with identifying the intellectual potential of children and constructed a series of tasks which increased in difficulty and complexity. Binet and Simon reasoned that it should be possible to develop tasks that could be completed by typical children of a specific age. For example, it should be possible to develop a number of tasks that can be completed by a typical six-year-old, but are beyond the ability of a typical five-year-old.

Binet and Simon devised a series of tests which did just that. Their tests were divided into different age levels which corresponded to the performance of a typical child of that age. The term mental age is used to describe a person's performance on the tests. If a five-year-old correctly answered the same questions as a typical seven-year-old, it would be said that he or she had a mental age of seven. Likewise, if an eight-year-old answered questions in the same way as a typical six-year-old, it would be said that he or she had a mental age of six.

For the majority of children their mental age will be the same as their chronological age (CA), their age in years. In order to make comparisons between individuals, a simple formula was developed which generates a person's IQ. A child's IQ is calculated by dividing their mental age by their chronological age and multiplying the result by 100. For example, if a ten-year-old girl had a mental age of 12 her IQ would be $\frac{12}{10} \times 100 = 120$. People of average intelligence will have an IQ of 100.

see also...

Intelligence; Psychological Tests; Quantitative and Qualitative; Reliability and Validity

Interpersonal Attraction

Why do we spend more time with some people than others? Why are we attracted to some people and not others? These are some of the questions addressed by psychologists carrying out research into interpersonal attraction.

There are a number of factors that can influence whether or not we are attracted to people. One of the most important factors in determining our initial attraction to another person is their physical attractiveness. People tend to choose partners whose level of physical attractiveness is similar to their own. In doing this people seem to be balancing the risks of rejection with an attempt to maximize the attractiveness of their prospective partner. However, what is considered to be attractive varies from person to person and from culture to culture. The extent to which other people share similar attitudes and beliefs to ourselves influences our choice of friends and acquaintances. People tend to like spending time with people who share similar views of the world. However, in close relationships people often prefer being with people whose strengths and needs complement their own. For example, submissive people often tend to prefer interacting with people who are more dominant.

When it comes to choosing a partner, a person's experiences as a child within his or her family background can be influential. Attachment theory suggests that a person's model of relationships develops in childhood and subsequently forms the basis of expectations about the quality of relationships with others. So people tend to be attracted to people whose behaviours and attitudes seem to be compatible with their own model of relationships. The views of families and friends can also be extremely influential in determining the course of relationships. For example, research investigating inter-ethnic relationships found that the approval or disapproval of friends and relatives was an important factor predicting dating behaviour.

see also...

Attachment; Gender Development; Intimate Relationships; Stereotypes

Intimate Relationships

It has been suggested that nearly everyone has a need for close personal relationships, that is intimate relationships, with other people. One model proposes that there are five stages in the development of an intimate relationship. The first stage comprises the initiation of the relationship and is followed by a period of exploration and finding common ground. This is followed by stage in which the level of commitment increases and the pair start to develop forms of communication that are unique to that relationship. In the next stage the two people become identifiable as a couple both to themselves and to other people. Finally, according to this model, the highest level of intimacy comes in the form of a public declaration of a commitment, for example through an engagement or marriage.

In most Western cultures one of the most common reasons people give for being committed to a long-term relationship is being in love. But what is love? One distinction has been made between passionate love and companionate love. Passionate love is characteristic of the early stages of a relationship, whereas companionate love grows over time as a result of shared experiences and is characterized by emotional intimacy and emotional closeness.

Robert Sternberg has proposed a triangular theory which proposes love has three key components: commitment, intimacy and passion. Sternberg suggests that these three components can be combined in different ways to produce eight different kinds of love, which he calls infatuated love, friendship, empty love, romantic love, companionate love, fatuous love, consummate love and nonlove. Romantic love is characterized by high levels of passion and intimacy but low levels of commitment, whereas empty love is low on passion and intimacy, but high on commitment. According to Sternberg, the most satisfying form of love is consummate love which is high on all three components.

see also...

Gender and Sex; Impression Formation; Interpersonal Attraction; Social Psychology

James, William

William James was born in New York City in 1842. He trained for a career in medicine and completed his studies while still living with his parents in Cambridge, Massachusetts. He spent most of his working life as a professor at Harvard University.

In 1890 James's interest in psychology resulted in the publication of a two-volume text called *The Principles of Psychology*. This was a hugely popular text and soon became the best-selling English language psychology text. One of the ideas William James developed in his book was a theory of emotion that has become known as the James-Lange theory of emotion. The theory suggests that our experience of emotion has its roots in our bodily experience. Consider the following situation. A man is walking down a dark street late at night and is confronted by a youth with a knife. The man runs away. The usual explanation given for an episode like this is that the man ran away because he was frightened. However, James proposed an alternative account. He suggested that our nervous system responds to threatening events by preparing us for action, and we then interpret these bodily responses in emotional terms. So James would argue that the man didn't run away because he was frightened, but rather he interpreted the bodily sensations associated with running away as fear.

Another influential idea developed by James was in the area of memory. He proposed a distinction between two types of memory; secondary memory which holds the vast store of factual information and personal memories we have accumulated during our lives, and primary memory which brings that information into our conscious awareness. William James has had a lasting impact on psychology. He provided the inspiration for an approach to psychology called functionalism which focuses on the role, or function, that psychological processes play in helping individuals adapt to their environment.

see also...

Emotion; Freud, Sigmund; Memory; Lewin, Kurt

Job Satisfaction

Angela works in a factory making running shoes. Her friend is thinking about applying for a job at the factory so she asks Angela what it is like to work there. Angela says, 'Every day it's the same thing over and over again. I do the same ten things every minute of every day. I've done it so often it's automatic so I often daydream when I'm working. But if you miss anything the supervisors shout at you and make you look small in front of the other workers. I hope I don't have to work there many more years. I'm fed up with it. I'd much rather stay at home and do the housework.'

Job satisfaction refers to people's feelings about the different aspects of their jobs and is usually measured using some form of questionnaire. Angela is clearly unhappy with her job, but what is it that makes people like or dislike their jobs? Several studies have found that people in the same jobs and working under similar conditions can have very different levels of job satisfaction. This has led some researchers to suggest that it is a combination of personal factors and characteristics of the job that influence the extent to which people are satisfied with their jobs.

Hackman and Oldham suggest that there are certain job characteristics that are associated with levels of satisfaction. These include skill variety, task identity, job feedback and autonomy. If we consider Angela's job, it is repetitive, (low skill variety), she is responsible only for one part of the whole shoe-making process (low task identity), she has very little discretion over how she goes about doing the job (low autonomy) and she gets feedback only when she does something wrong (low job feedback). It is therefore not very surprising that she is unhappy in her job. There is some evidence that job satisfaction is related to personality, in that some people are predisposed to like their jobs whereas other people are predisposed to dislike them, regardless of the job.

see also...

Attitudes; Motivation; Stress; Survey; Work and Organizational Psychology

Jung, Carl Gustav

Carl Gustav Jung was born in 1875 in the small Swiss village of Kessewil. After graduating from the University of Basel he took up a career in psychiatry. He was already an admirer of the work of Sigmund Freud when they met in Vienna in 1907. A friendship quickly developed between the two and at one point it seemed that Jung would follow in the footsteps of Freud. However, as time went on they began to disagree on a number of issues and ultimately the differences of opinion became so great that they parted company. Jung died in Zurich in 1961 aged 85.

After the split with Freud, Jung went on to develop his own theory of personality. According to Jung a person's personality is composed of three interacting systems: consciousness (often referred to as the 'ego'), the personal unconscious and the collective unconscious. Jung used the term 'psyche' to refer to the totality of these interacting parts. Consciousness is the part of the mind that individuals are aware of. The personal unconscious is made up of repressed memories and experiences that did not reach the level of consciousness. Jung believed that the personal unconscious is organised into clusters that function as separate units. He called these clusters complexes.

The second layer of the unconscious, the collective unconscious, represents Jung's acknowledgement of the role of evolution in determining people's current experience of the world. He proposed that because we all share a common evolutionary history we have deep-rooted tendencies to interpret the world in similar ways. Jung used the term archetypes to refer to these inherited tendencies to perceive experiences in particular ways. He believed that our personality, our psyche, is present from birth and is not acquired in a piecemeal fashion as the result of our experiences in the world. He also believed that our aim in life is to maintain the wholeness of our psyche and prevent it from splitting up into separate and conflicting parts.

see also...

Defence Mechanisms; Freud, Sigmund; Psychotherapy; Repression

Kohler, Wolfgang

Wolfgang Kohler was born in 1887 near the Baltic Sea in East Prussia. He trained as a psychologist at the University of Berlin and died in 1967. Kohler is credited with being one of the three founding members of the Gestalt approach to psychology. The other two were Max Wertheimer and Kurt Koffka. In 1935 Kohler left Germany to take up a position at Swarthmore College in the United States, where he worked until his retirement. During his time in America he became the major spokesman for the Gestalt movement and was elected President of the American Psychological Association in 1959.

In 1913 he went to Canary Islands to work at a primate research facility on the island of Tenerife where he remained until 1920. During his time on Tenerife he carried out research into the problem-solving behaviour of chimpanzees. At the time it was believed that humans and animals solve problems through a process of trial and error. Kohler's work was to provide an innovative alternative to thinking about problem solving. His theory was based on observations of the way in which chimpanzees solved problems. A typical problem might involve placing some fruit just out of the chimp's reach, but leaving some sticks lying around the cage. What Kohler noticed in experiments like this was that the chimp would attempt to get the fruit by reaching through the bars. When this failed there would be a period of little or no activity when it appeared that the chimp had given up on the problem. Then there would be a sudden burst of activity as the chimp grabbed one of the sticks and started to poke it through the bars to reach the fruit. Kohler used the term 'insight' to refer to the chimp's discovery. This flash of insight, when the answer to a problem suddenly comes to us, is often referred to as the 'aha' phenomenon. Kohler suggested that during the quiet period prior to solving the problem the chimp was restructuring the problem.

Kohler's work with chimps set the agenda for subsequent work with humans.

see also...

Cognitive Psychology;
Comparative Psychology; Gestalt
Psychology; Problem Solving

Language Development

Jacqueline's parents made lots of home videos of her while she was growing up. One night they decided to sit down and watch some of them. One of the things they noticed was how quickly Jacqueline's language skills developed in the first few years of her life. When she was about six months old she had begun to babble and was putting together strings of syllables like 'da-da-da-da' and 'ba-ba-ba-ba'. By the time she was a year old Jacqueline was uttering single words like 'no', 'juice' and 'more'. Jacqueline's parents laughed when they remembered she went through a phase of calling anything with four legs a 'doggie' and all adult males were 'dadda'. These kinds of errors are common in children and are referred to as overextension errors. When she was 30 months old Jacqueline was able to combine words to form two word utterances such as 'eat cookie', 'doggy run' and 'more juice'. By the time she reached the age of five Jacqueline was using grammatically correct sentences containing many different ideas. It has been estimated that by the age of six years a typical child will have a vocabulary of approximately 14,000 words. Jacqueline is a typical child and her language development is similar to that of most other children.

There are a number of theories which attempt to explain how we acquire language. The two most notable accounts are those of Burrhus F. Skinner and Noam Chomsky. Skinner proposed that language is learned through a process of reward or reinforcement. When a baby utters sounds that resemble words, they are likely to be rewarded by the parents, for example, by the use of smiles or hugs. This increases the likelihood of the sounds being repeated. So language acquisition is dependent on the environment. Chomsky, on the other hand, proposed that children are born with a set of brain structures specialized for the acquisition of language. In other words children have an innate language acquisition device which facilitates the process of language development.

see also...

Chomsky, Noam; Conditioning; Developmental Psychology; Non-Verbal Communication; Skinner, Burrhus F.

Leadership

Most people in work are either leaders themselves or are on the receiving end of a leader's actions and behaviour. The topic of leadership is concerned with the personal qualities, styles and behaviours of a leader. There are two key questions when considering the nature of leadership. First, can we identify and describe effective leaders? Second, can we distinguish effect leaders from ineffective ones?

Numerous models and theories have been developed in an attempt to determine how effective leaders differ from ineffective ones. One approach has attempted to look for the answer in terms of personality traits, but no consistent patterns have emerged. Indeed, it has been found on many occasions that people with different traits can be successful in the same situation. Another approach has focused on the behaviours of leaders, in other words, what they do and how they do it. Research carried out at Ohio State University identified two types of behaviour which effective leaders can use to help groups achieve their goals. First, effective leaders focus the attention of the group on task-related issues such as the quality and quantity of the work produced. Secondly, effective leaders are considerate and supportive of team members, for example, in helping them achieve personal goals, such as promotion and job satisfaction. However, one of the problems of behavioural models is that they tend to neglect the effects of the situation within which the leadership behaviour is taking place.

Fred Fiedler and his colleagues developed a model of leadership which looked at the relationship between the personal characteristics and behaviours of leaders and the nature of the situation they were working in. For example, Fiedler would argue that if they are to be effective, a Colonel in the army and a college principal need to behave differently and have different characteristics because they are working in entirely different situations.

see also...

Groups; Lewin, Kurt; Job Satisfaction; Work and Organizational Psychology

Levels of Processing

Emma and Melanie are revising for their French exam. Melanie is trying to learn her French vocabulary by reading the words over and over in the hope that she will be able to remember them in the exam. Emma has adopted a slightly different approach and is trying to understand the meanings of the words and establish similarities and relationships between different words. Although they both passed the exam, Emma did rather better than Melanie.

The majority of theories on human memory see it in terms of a number of different stores. For example, a distinction is made between a long-term memory store, which contains information covering the whole of our lives, and a short-term memory store that holds information for relatively brief periods of time. Fergus Craik and Robert Lockhart proposed an alternative approach to thinking about memory. They suggested that whether or not we remember something depends on the processes that take place at the time of learning. They proposed that we can process information at different levels, ranging from deep to shallow. They also suggested that the deeper we process information the more likely we are to remember it. The deepest level of processing focuses on the meaning of the information, whereas at a shallow level we simply focus on the physical characteristics of the information. In the example above Emma was processing information more deeply than Melanie because she was paying attention to the meanings of the words rather than trying to learn them by rote.

Although deeper processing usually results in better recall there are other factors which can affect the ease with which people can recall information. People are more likely to remember information if the context within which they are trying to recall the information is the same as when they originally learned it. The fact that a match between learning and retrieval conditions enhances performance is known as the encoding specificity principle.

see also...

Cognitive Psychology; Episodic, Semantic and Procedural Memory; Forgetting; Memory

Lewin, Kurt

Kurt Lewin was one of the many European psychologists who emigrated to the United States to escape persecution by the Nazis in Germany. He was born in Germany in 1890 and was awarded his doctorate in 1914. After World War I, he became involved with the Gestalt psychology group in Berlin led by Wolfgang Kohler. In 1935 he settled in the United States and spent nine years working at the University of Iowa. In 1944 he moved to the Massachusetts Institute of Technology to become Director of a research centre. He died in 1947.

Lewin used many of the principles derived from Gestalt psychology in an attempt to develop a theory of personality and social behaviour. His approach, which has been referred to as field theory, suggests that we need to understand a person's behaviour in terms of their interaction with the environment. Lewin used the notion of a life space which comprises the person in their psychological environment. In contrast to psychodynamic theories which propose that our behaviour is governed by our past events, Lewin argued that when we are trying to understand behaviour we need to focus on the present situation and the events which are currently taking place. In other words, only the present can cause present behaviour. One of his famous quotes is, 'There's nothing so practical as a good theory.' By this he meant that many of the theories developed in psychology can be very useful in solving practical problems.

Lewin was also responsible for developing an approach to research called action research. Psychologists are often involved in research which is concerned with promoting change in social settings and organizations, where it is not always desirable or helpful for the researcher to maintain their distance from the phenomena being researched. Lewin's model of action research addresses these problems through an ongoing cycle of planning, acting, observing and reflecting.

see also...

Experimental Method; Gestalt Psychology; Personality; Psychodynamic Approaches; Social Psychology

Memory

Imagine for a minute what life might be like if we couldn't remember things that have happened to us, recognize people and places we know well, or recall the sequence of actions necessary to make a cup of tea. Life as we know it would be impossible if we couldn't remember things from one day to the next. However, there are some people, usually as a result of either injury or disease, who suffer from this form of extreme memory loss (amnesia). Consider the following activities: looking up a telephone number and remembering it until you have dialled, recalling some event of your primary school days, riding a bike, knowing that Paris is the capital of France. These are very different activities and models of our memory processes must be able to account for them all.

In recent years the most influential model of memory is one proposed by Richard Atkinson and Richard Shiffrin in the late 1960s. This model draws on the computer analogy and conceptualizes memory in terms of information moving between different stores. One of these stores is referred to as the Short-Term Store (STS). This is the memory store that can hold a telephone number for the short period of time between looking it up in the directory and dialling the number. It is seen as holding information on a temporary basis and having a limited capacity. A classic study carried out by George Miller in the 1950s suggested that the capacity of our STS is approximately seven items. We can hold information in the STS by the process of rehearsal, that is, continually repeating it over and over to ourselves, otherwise the information held there is displaced by new information coming in.

According to Atkinson and Shiffrin rehearsal is the process by which information is transferred from the STS to the Long-Term Store (LTS). In contrast to the limited capacity STS, the LTS is seen as permanent store with a more or less unlimited capacity.

see also...

Episodic, Semantic and Procedural Memory; Schemas and Scripts; Primacy and Recency Effects

Milgram, Stanley

The American psychologist Stanley Milgram (1933–84) is best remembered for his work on the reasons why people obey an authority figure. One the key questions is: How do people react if they are asked by a person in authority to do something that they know is wrong? Unfortunately, the twentieth century is full of examples of atrocities being committed by people who were only following orders. For example, in 1968 several hundred unarmed civilians in the South Vietnamese village of My Lai were massacred by three platoons of American soldiers. The soldiers were following the orders of their commanding officer. In the Second World War millions of prisoners, many of them Jewish, died at the hands of German soldiers in concentration camps.

In the 1960s Milgram conducted a series of classic studies investigating obedience to authority. He set up an experimental situation that involved asking people to administer electric shocks to someone else. In fact the person supposedly receiving the shock was an actor and the apparatus didn't actually deliver a shock. The amazing finding to come out of Milgram's studies was that many ordinary people would administer electric shocks that were appearing to cause the victim extreme pain and were potentially deadly. However, many participants were extremely distressed by the experience and his experiments raised a number of ethical issues surrounding the treatment of participants in psychological research.

There are a number of factors which can account for the reasons why people tend to obey, even though it results in harm to others. In many situations the person carrying out the orders takes no responsibility for the consequences of their actions. It is assumed that the responsibility lies with the person giving the commands. In addition, individuals often find it difficult to disobey authority figures who are displaying visible signs of their status.

see also...

Asch, Solomon; Attitudes; Bandura, Albert; Groups; Social Psychology

Moral Development

Understanding the values of the society within which we live and regulating our behaviour accordingly are important aspects of an individual's development. A child's concept of what is right and wrong changes as he or she grows older and research into moral development focuses on this process of change.

One of the most influential theories of moral development has been developed by the American psychologist, Lawrence Kohlberg. Kohlberg studied with Jean Piaget and was heavily influenced by his ideas. Kohlberg carried out much of his research into moral development by using moral dilemmas. A typical dilemma forced the participant to make a choice between either upholding the law or breaking the law in favour of some humanitarian action. For example, in one dilemma a man has a sick wife who is dying from cancer. There is a drug that can save her but the company who produce it are charging $2,000 for it even though it only costs $200 to make. The man tries to borrow some money but can raise only $1,000. He goes to the company and tells them that his wife is dying and asks them to sell him the drug more cheaply or let him pay later. The company refuse. The man gets desperate and breaks into the company to steal the drug for his wife. In dilemmas like this there are arguments for and against the man stealing the drug.

On the basis of how children responded to such dilemmas, Kohlberg developed his theory of moral development. He proposed that children progress through three levels of moral development. At the first level, pre-conventional morality, children judge right or wrong by the consequences of actions. At the second level, conventional morality, the views of other people and the intentions behind an action become much more important. At the final level, post-conventional morality, it becomes recognized that there is often a distinction between what is legally right and what is morally right.

see also...

Cognitive Development; Developmental Psychology; Piaget, Jean; Social Development

Motivation

Nobody at Allbits manufacturing company knew what to do about Rob Smith. Rob worked in the Research and Development department and part of his job was to evaluate the feasibility of research proposals. During the last couple of years there have been a number of complaints about the speed, or rather the lack of it, with which Rob processed the proposals. Because of his background and skills it would be difficult to move Rob to another department. Is there anything Rob's boss can do to improve his performance at work?

Motivation is an important topic in work and organizational psychology and is concerned with the factors that influence the way we behave in the workplace. There are a number of theories which attempt to explain motivation in terms of psychological needs. The basic premise behind these theories is that we behave in ways which are aimed at satisfying our needs. One of the earliest and best known need theories was developed by Abraham Maslow. He proposed that there are five categories of human needs: biological, for example, food and drink; safety,

for example, a physically secure environment; belonginess, for example, the need to feel close to another person; esteem needs, for example, the need to feel valued and respected by friends and family; self-actualization, for example, the need to develop our skills and fulfil our potential. One of the main implications of Maslow's theory for the motivation of employees is that it is essential to know what needs the individual is trying to satisfy.

An alternative approach to motivation is taken by goal setting theory developed by Ed Locke and his colleagues in the United States. Goal setting theory is based on the observation that when people start a task they invariably keep going until they complete it. According to this theory, setting Rob relatively difficult but specific goals would be likely to produce an improvement in his performance.

see also...

Job Satisfaction; Social Psychology; Work and Organizational Psychology

Neurons

Our bodies are made up of billions of cells. Each cell in our body has evolved to perform a particular function. For example, muscle cells contract, red blood cells carry oxygen around the body and nerve cells transmit information. Nerve cells that make up our nervous system are called neurons.

Although neurons come in many different shapes and sizes, they are typically long and thin and each neuron has connections with thousands of other neurons. The connections between neurons are called synapses and consist of a tiny fluid-filled space called the synaptic gap. Information is passed across the synaptic gap by means of chemicals called neurotransmitters. Neurotransmitters are released by the neuron on one side of the synaptic gap and picked up by special receptor sites on the other neuron. One of the key characteristics of neurons is their ability to conduct electrical charges from one end of the cell to the other. It is this mechanism which enables information to be transferred from one neuron to another. If a neuron receives sufficient stimulation from other neurons it causes an electric current to travel along the length of the neuron. This process is referred to as the 'firing' of the neuron. This firing happens on an 'all or none' basis. In other words there is a threshold below which the neuron will not fire, but once the stimulation from other neurons reaches a certain level the neuron will fire. When a neuron fires it results in the release of neurotransmitters at its synapses. When neurotransmitters are picked up at another neuron's receptor sites it has the effect of stimulating the neuron and, if it receives sufficient stimulation, it will fire as well.

There are three basic types of neuron. Sensory neurons convey information to our brain. Motor neurons transmit information from our brain to other parts of our body, and interneurons connect neurons with one another.

see also...

Biological Psychology; Brain Structure; Neurotransmitters; Schizophrenia

Neurotransmitters

Mind-altering drugs have been used throughout the history of human civilization. These drugs were used well before we had any understanding of how they actually worked. People used them because of the effect they produced. However, research into the chemistry of the brain has enabled us to understand their effects in terms of neurotransmitters operating in the brain.

Neurotransmitters are the chemicals that enable nerve cells (neurons) to transmit information to one another. Neurons in the brain are connected to each other by a small fluid filled gap called a synapse. Neurotransmitters released by one neuron cross the synapse and are picked up by receptors on the other neuron. As a general rule each neuron will release only one type of neurotransmitter, so it is possible to label the neuron by the neurotransmitter it uses. Serotonin, dopamine, noradrenaline and acetylcholine are four neurotransmitters that have been studied extensively. Dopamine, for example, is a neurotransmitter that has been implicated in a range of different phenomena. A number of so-called recreational drugs, such as marijuana, appear to increase the release of dopamine in the brain and it has been suggested that the addictive quality of drugs such as heroin is, in part, related to this process. Dopamine is also implicated in Parkinson's disease. This is a degenerative disorder characterized by uncontrollable body tremors and difficulty in starting or stopping movements such as walking. Parkinson's disease is associated with damage to a part of the brain which is involved in the production of dopamine.

Depression has been associated with decreased levels of the neurotransmitter serotonin. Antidepressants also work by their actions on neurotransmitters. Prozac, for example, works by increasing the levels of serotonin in the brain.

see also...

Biopsychology; Brain Structure; Clinical Psychology; Depression; Neurons

Non-Verbal Communication

Your friend Mark has just been to the clinic for a check-up. As he comes into the room you look at him and even before he speaks you know something is wrong. We communicate with other people in a variety of ways including talking to them, writing to them and also by using non-verbal cues. But what were the cues we might have picked up from Mark when he entered the room?

We can identify a number of non-verbal channels that are used to express our feelings. These include facial expressions, eye contact, body language and touching. It has been suggested that anger, fear, happiness, sadness, surprise and disgust are six basic emotions that can be expressed by the human face. However, this doesn't mean that people are capable only of expressing six emotions. In reality emotions occur in many different combinations, for example, we can be surprised and disgusted at the same time or we can feel angry and frightened. So there are an enormous number of expressions that people can use based on a combination of the six basic emotions.

Eye contact plays an important role in facilitating the smooth flow of a conversation between two people. The person speaking tends to avoid eye contact until they are near the end of their utterance, at which point they will look at the other person. It seems that this acts as cue to inform the other person that they are about to finish talking. On the other hand the person listening usually maintains eye contact with the speaker. Eye contact is also used in other ways, for example, staring directly and continuously at another person is often seen as a sign of anger or hostility. Body language, the position and movements of our body, can communicate a lot of information about our state of mind. For example, sitting with arms and legs crossed can indicate a defensive posture. Touching is the most intimate non-verbal cue and whether or not it is considered appropriate depends very much on the context.

see also...

Attitudes; Impression Formation; Language Development; Social Psychology

Parapsychology

athew had just broken up with his girlfriend and was feeling as if he would never be able to sustain a long-term relationship. One of the things he wanted out of life was to be able to settle down and have a family. He didn't know what to do next. As he was walking home he noticed a card in newsagent's window advertising tarot card readings. That was it! He decided there and then that this was the way to get some answers to his questions. The next day Mathew contacted the tarot card reader and made an appointment to have his cards read. Sarah was taking her driving test in the morning and was extremely apprehensive about it. She had taken countless driving lessons and the driving instructor was confident that she would pass her test. On the morning of her test Sarah got dressed and opened the drawer of her dressing table. She took out a small toy mouse called Squimp – it was her good luck charm. Things always went well when she had Squimp to look after her. Sarah and Mathew are examples of people who believe in the paranormal.

Parapsychologists investigate paranormal beliefs and experiences using psychological methods and principles. The term psi (pronounced 'sigh') phenomena is used to describe events that appear to defy the established laws of science. Extrasensory perception (ESP) is an example of the type of phenomena investigated by parapsychologists. It is argued that there are four types of ESP: clairvoyance, telepathy, precognition and psychokinesis. Clairvoyance is the ability to perceive events or objects in ways that do not rely on the normal senses. Telepathy refers to the ability to transfer thoughts directly from one person to another without using any of the normal means of communication. Precognition is the ability to see and predict the future; and psychokinesis is the ability to move objects using thought alone. The majority of psychologists are still sceptical about the existence of ESP and related phenomena.

see also...

Attitudes; Experimental Method; Significance Testing; Social Psychology

Perception

As Shakila was walking down the country lane she could smell the lavender blossom, hear the birds singing and as she looked into the fields she could see horses running towards her. Perception is concerned with how we make use of the information that comes from our sense organs such as our eyes, noses, and ears. What we see, smell, hear and touch is referred to as our perceptual experience.

One of the problems faced by psychologists is to explain how the input to our sensory systems is converted into the sights, sounds, smells, and tastes we experience. Just stop for a minute and think about what you were doing for the 30 minutes before you started reading this book. How many different ways were you perceiving the environment? How many different senses did you make use of?

For most of us, our perceptual experience of the world is not something we consciously reflect on. Our experience of the world is usually so immediate and direct that we just take it for granted. However, if we consider what is involved in visual perception we will soon become aware of the complexity of the processes involved. Our vision is based on the light that enters our eyes. The eye is a spherical object with a lens at the front and a layer of nerve cells, the retina, covering its rear surface. The nerve cells that make up the retina are light sensitive and are connected to the visual cortex, which is the part of the brain that processes visual information, via the optic nerve. The retina is a flat curved surface, which leads to the first problem confronting psychologists, namely, how does this two-dimensional image on our retina become transformed into the three-dimensional representation of the world which is our perceptual experience? However, we cannot fully understand these processes simply by relying on an analysis of our biological systems. Our beliefs and expectations can also exert a considerable influence on what we perceive.

see also...

Biological Psychology; Cognitive Psychology; Neurons; Schizophrenia

Personality

Personality refers to distinctive patterns of behaviour which characterize the way a person behaves in different situations. After they have finished their lunch Angie and Jane are sitting having a coffee when a passing waiter trips and spills a drink over them. Jane jumps up and shouts at the waiter, whereas Angie picks up a napkin to wipe her clothes and says to the waiter, 'It's OK, accidents happen'. Different people respond differently to similar events.

Research into personality has two main goals. The first is concerned with differences between people and aims to identify those differences that are psychologically important. A second goal is concerned with understanding those differences and using them as a way of predicting how people will behave in different situations. Will Angie and Jane behave in a similar way in different situations? For example, in dealing with a customer's complaint will Jane respond in an aggressive manner and Angie in a supportive and understanding manner? These are the kinds of questions asked by personality psychologists.

There are a number of different approaches to personality taken within psychology. Two of the major approaches are the psychodynamic approach and the trait approach. The psychodynamic approach has its roots in the writings of Sigmund Freud. It focuses on personality as an unconscious struggle between various forces in the mind. It assumes that a person's problems are the consequence of these underlying conflicts. On the other hand, the trait approach assumes that people have a set of underlying tendencies, or traits, to behave in a certain way across different situations. So someone who has a friendly trait will tend to be friendly across a whole range of situations. Hans Eysenck's theory of personality is an example of a trait theory. He suggested that personality could be described in terms of three major traits which he called extraversion, neuroticism, and psychotism.

see also...

Eysenck, Hans; Freud, Sigmund; Impression Formation; Intelligence; Social Pychology

Piaget, Jean

Jean Piaget (1896–1980 studied natural sciences at the University of Neuchâtel where he obtained a PhD. One of the questions that interested Piaget throughout his long career was: How does knowledge grow? Piaget believed that cognitive development progressed as a result of the child interacting with the environment. He suggested that cognitive development in childhood progresses through a series of stages.

The first of these stages, the 'sensorimotor stage', covers approximately the first two years of a child's life. During this stage children learn about the world by physically interacting with it. Objects are grasped, put in the mouth and sometimes thrown around! If an object is hidden from view children below the age of 12 months will bahave as if it no longer exists. A major achievement in this stage is to recognize that objects still exist even if we cannot see them. The second stage is the 'preoperational stage' that begins around the age of two and lasts until the age of six or seven. During this stage children develop the ability to solve problems through thinking rather than having to physically manipulate objects. The third stage, the 'concrete operational' stage, lasts roughly from the age of seven to twelve and is characterized by children's ability to understand the concept of conservation. The classic illustration of conservation is to pour liquid from a short fat container into a tall thin one. Children who can conserve will recognize that the amount of liquid is unchanged, whereas children who can't conserve will not. The final stage is the 'formal operational stage' which begins between the ages of twelve and fifteen. This stage is characterized by the ability to manipulate abstract ideas as well as concrete objects and events. Some of Piaget's specific ideas have been criticized by other psychologists, but his broad principles have withstood the test of time.

see also...

*Cognitive Development;
Developmental Psychology; Moral
Development; Social Development*

Play

Throughout their childhood years, children spend a lot of their time either playing on their own or with others. The Swiss psychologist, Jean Piaget, proposed that children's intellectual development progresses through a series of stages. He also argued that the type of play children engage in corresponds to their stage of development.

According to Piaget, up to the age of two years children engage in mastery or practice play. This involves repetition of newly learned activities, such as shaking a toy that makes a noise. Activities such as this help children to develop their motor skills and their hand-eye coordination. Between the ages of two years and seven, children begin to engage more often in make-believe and pretend play. Piaget used the term symbolic play to describe this type of play. From the age of seven, children begin to play more elaborate games which are governed by quite specific rules.

Although children are encouraged to play and certain types of play have an important role in nursery and infant school curriculum, the exact role that play has in a child's development remains unclear. It has been suggested that pretend play can help children to develop an understanding of the way in which other people see the world. Three different forms of pretend play have been identified. The first involves using one object to represent another, for example, sitting in a cardboard box and pretending it is a boat. The second type involves pretending that things have certain attributes or properties, for example, pretending that a doll is tired and wants to go to bed. The third type involves the use of imaginary objects, for example, pretending to drink tea from an empty cup.

Another form of play commonly observed in school playgrounds is 'rough-and-tumble' play. It involves physical contact, such as wrestling, grappling and rolling around on the ground.

see also...

Cognitive Development; Developmental Psychology; Moral Development; Piaget, Jean; Social Development

Post-Traumatic Stress Disorder

Zara had been working in a shop selling expensive jewellery for a couple of years. One Thursday in June two men walked into the shop and pulled sawn-off shotguns out of their coats. Zara's boss, the owner of the shop, tried to raise the alarm but one of the gunmen shot him at point blank range. The other man pressed the shotgun into Zara's face and shouted at her to put the money and jewellery into a bag. Zara couldn't stop shaking with fear but she managed to do as she was told. The gunman struck her on the head with his gun and both men ran out of the shop. Zara's boss was dead when the paramedics arrived.

A couple of months later Zara's head injuries had healed, but she was experiencing many other problems. She was having difficulty getting to sleep at night and suffered from a lack of concentration. Zara hasn't been back to work since the robbery and she avoided going anywhere near the shop where it happened. Before the robbery Zara used to enjoy going out with her friends, dining out and going to the cinema. Since the robbery she's only been out with her friends a couple of times and hasn't really enjoyed it. Perhaps one of the most distressing problems for Zara is that she can't stop thinking about the robbery and she can't get the horrific images of her boss being shot out of her mind. Zara is suffering from post-traumatic stress disorder (PTSD).

The symptoms of PTSD usually appear shortly after the trauma, although in some cases it can appear several months after the traumatic event. As you might expect, PTSD is relatively common in soldiers who experience combat. For example, the Vietnam war left many American soldiers suffering from PTSD. One account of PTSD suggests that many of the problems people experience occur because they are not able to incorporate the information about the traumatic event into their existing schemas. As a result, the information about the event repeatedly finds its way into our conscious awareness in the form of flashbacks and vivid imagery.

see also...

Cognitive Psychology; Emotion; Memory; Schemas and Scripts; Stress

Prejudice

ngela had just arrived at work and the first thing she said to her friend was, 'Old people are useless. I really don't like them. They can't drive, they can't do anything. They should have their licences taken off them when they reach 65.' Her friend was really taken aback by this statement and decided that she should have a long talk with Angela about her attitude towards old people. Angela is prejudiced against old people. She is expressing a dislike of old people simply because they are old.

A person who is prejudiced typically dislikes other people simply because they belong to a particular social group. Although prejudice usually implies a negative evaluation of others, in some cases prejudice can be positive. In other words a person is liked simply because they belong to a particular social group. If Angela deliberately treated old people worse than other people she would be guilty of discrimination. Discrimination refers to a behaviour or action, whereas prejudice is an attitude toward the members of a social group. But why are people prejudiced?

Social identity theory, developed by Henri Tajfel, suggests that one of the main ways in which we develop a sense of identity is through these groups we belong to. We all belong to a number of different groups, for example, a racial group, a work group, a group based on our gender, and a religious group. Each of these groups provides us with a different social identity. Social identity theory also suggests that we have a need to see the groups to which we belong as being better than other similar groups. The more we can see the groups to which we belong in a positive light the better we feel about ourselves. According to social identity theory it is this need to make comparisons with other groups which can lead to prejudice and discrimination.

Is it possible to overcome prejudice? One approach has achieved some success by bringing people together from different social groups to cooperate in the achievement of a common goal.

see also...

Attitudes; Impression Formation; Social Psychology; Stereotypes

Primacy and Recency Effects

Heidi has just started dating Shaun. Shaun has been in trouble with the police; nothing serious, he was caught shoplifting when he was a young teenager. He hasn't been in any trouble since then. Shaun has lots of good points, he is polite, kind, amusing and thoughtful. Heidi knows she should tell her mother about Shaun's shoplifting, but should she tell her the good things about him first? Does the order in which we hear information make any difference to our judgements?

Solomon Asch investigated the effect of presenting information in different ways on people's judgements. He described a person using a list of words, half of which were positive, for example, industrious and the other half negative, for example, envious. In his study, Asch gave one group of people the positive words first and another group the negative words first. When the people in the study were asked to rate the person being described, those who had heard the positive words first formed a more favourable impression than those who had heard the negative words first. This showed that the information presented first had more impact on people's judgements than information presented later. This effect has been called the primacy effect. So if Heidi wants her mother to form a good impression about Shaun she would be best advised to tell her mother the good things about him first!

A primacy effect is also obtained when people are given the task of recalling a list of words or numbers. For example, read the following fifteen numbers to a friend at the rate of about one per second and then ask them to see how many they can remember.

17, 21, 93, 36, 27, 41, 52, 84, 19, 68, 73, 45, 49, 37, 58

As well as remembering the first items on a list people will tend to remember the last few items on the list as well. This is referred to as the recency effect. However, the recency effect is less robust than the primacy effect and can be disrupted more easily.

see also...

Asch, Solomon; Impression Formation; Memory

Problem Solving

Estelle and her husband are considering moving to a larger house. But how much should they spend and what part of town should they move to? Carol and Bob wanted to eat out rather than cooking at home. Which restaurant should they go to? Should they eat Italian, Chinese, French, or go for a takeaway burger? People are confronted by numerous problems every day of their lives. Some of these problems are solved relatively easily, whereas others are rather more complex. Problem solving involves reaching a goal by changing the current situation. It is an activity with a purpose and a direction.

One of the factors that can influence how we solve problems is our previous experience. In some situations our previous experience can make it easier to solve current problems. This is referred to as 'positive transfer'. For example, Carol tries to start the car but the battery is flat and the engine won't turn over. She's had this problem before and knows exactly how to solve it. Carol keeps a pair of 'jump leads' in her car and she uses them to connect her battery to the battery in her husband's car. This enables her to get her car started. However, in other situations our past experience can actually inhibit our ability to solve problems. One example of this is referred to as 'functional fixedness', which refers to a tendency to think about objects in terms of their normal usage. One study presented people with the problem of attaching a candle to a vertical screen. They were given a box full of nails and some matches. In order to solve the problem it is necessary to empty the nails out of the box and use it as a platform for the candle. As a result of their past experience the majority of people saw the box simply as a container for the nails and failed to solve the problem. This is an example of 'negative transfer', where our previous experience inhibits our problem-solving ability.

see also...

*Cognitive Psychology;
Experimental Method; Memory;
Perception*

Pro-Social Behaviour

In the early hours of 13 March 1964, Kitty Genovese was returning home from work in New York City. As she got close to her apartment building, a man armed with a knife approached her. She tried to run away but the man ran after her, caught her and stabbed her. Kitty screamed for help and as the lights came on in the apartment building her attacker moved away. When no one came to help Kitty, he returned and stabbed her repeatedly until she was dead. The attack took 45 minutes. It was later determined that 38 people had witnessed the attack and none of them had intervened. Only one person telephoned the police. This news story of an actual crime provided the impetus for a considerable amount of research into pro-social behaviour.

Pro-social behaviour is another term for helping behaviour. It describes helpful behaviour that benefits another person but has no obvious benefit for the person doing the helping. One of the important questions posed by the Kitty Genovese case is why bystanders are sometimes helpful in an emergency and sometimes indifferent? John Darley and Bibb Latane conducted a number of studies into the factors influencing bystander intervention. They suggested that when there is a large number of bystanders or observers of a crime or situation where someone requires help, the responsibility to act is shared among all the observers. This is referred to as a diffusion of responsibility and the outcome is that no one intervenes because no one feels any personal responsibility. However, in situations where there is only one bystander, the responsibility for helping the victim falls firmly on to that person, and he or she is much more likely to intervene.

Darley and Latane point out that taking responsibility for acting is only one part of the process. Even if the bystander takes responsibility for helping, that person can't do anything useful if he or she doesn't have the skills necessary for an effective intervention.

see also...

Attitudes; Social Facilitation; Social Psychology; Stereotypes

Psychodynamic Approaches

Psychodynamic approaches within psychology stem from the writings of Sigmund Freud. Freud's ideas have inspired numerous psychologists, some of whom have followed his ideas closely while others have incorporated his ideas into their own theories. The term psychodynamic is a general term that encompasses those areas of psychology which assume that we are driven by the content of our unconscious minds. Most psychologists accept the notion that not all of our experiences are available to our conscious awareness. However, the Freudian idea of a dynamic unconscious, an unconscious that drives us and motivates us to behave in particular ways, is less well received by many psychologists outside the psychodynamic tradition. The terms psychoanalysis and psychanalytic are reserved for Freud's original ideas on therapy and his theory of the human mind.

An important idea in the psychodynamic approach is the view that our childhood experiences have a considerable influence on our behaviour as adults. For example, Mike was attracted to exciting, outgoing and successful women, but when he did manage to establish a relationship with such a woman he soon lost interest and the relationship ended. This pattern repeated itself over and over again, so much so that Mike went to see a psychotherapist. It emerged during therapy that Mike's mother was a highly successful businesswoman who paid him little attention during his childhood. As an adult he was attracted to women similar to his mother but was also afraid that they would reject him as his mother had done. The psychodynamic approach assumes that virtually none of our behaviour is accidental. All behaviour is motivated and goal directed, although we may not be consciously aware of the goals and the driving forces behind the behaviour.

Psychodynamic approaches have given rise to a number of theories of personality development and different forms of therapy.

see also...

Clinical Psychology; Freud, Sigmund; Jung, Carl; Personality; Psychotherapy

Psychological Tests

How can you measure an individual's personality, their intelligence, reading ability, spatial ability or any other mental ability? One way would be to use one of the numerous tests psychologists have developed to measure a whole range of human abilities. These tests are often referred to as 'psychometric tests'.

Tests are used in many branches of psychology, particularly in clinical psychology and work and organizational psychology. In clinical psychology tests can be used as an aid to diagnosis. For example, clinical psychologists often see people who are suffering from some form of brain damage. When dealing with such clients it is important to identify which mental abilities have been impaired and which remain more or less intact. Psychological tests can play an important role in identifying the specific problems confronting people with brain damage. This information can then be used in designing appropriate treatment programmes.

Jack has been short-listed for a managerial position and has just found out that the selection process is going to take a full day. In the morning he will be completing some tests and in the afternoon he will be interviewed. Jack is a little concerned about the tests and he finds out more about them. Apparently he will be taking two tests – one concerned with personality and the other with mental ability. One of the assumptions underlying the use of psychological tests in this context is that performance on the tests is related to future job performance. If this is not the case then the test should not be used. A good test should be reliable and valid. In other words it should give the same results if administered to the same person on more than one occasion (reliable) and measure what it claims to measure (valid).

Psychological tests cannot be used by just anyone; the majority can be administered only by professional psychologists who have been trained in their use.

see also...

Clinical Psychology; Intelligence Quotient; Personality; Reliability and Validity; Work and Organizational Psychology

Psychotherapy

sychotherapy is a social interaction which takes place when a person seeks the help of a trained professional in order to change how they feel or behave. Psychotherapy differs from the support we get from friends and family when we are going through a difficult period in our lives, because it involves an interaction with a professional practitioner. There are many different forms of psychotherapy, but a broad distinction can be made between insight-oriented therapies and action-oriented therapies.

Insight-oriented therapies are aimed at helping people to understand the underlying source of their problems and include humanistic and psychodynamic. Action-oriented therapies such as cognitive behavioural therapy, take a more active role in helping people to change their behaviour and patterns of thinking. Although there are many differences between therapies there are also some issues about which there is a general agreement. For example, there is a general agreement that therapy is most likely to be effective when in takes place within a safe and caring context.

Therapy isn't always conducted with individuals, in many situations it is more appropriate to carry out therapy with a group of people. The group could be a number of unrelated clients selected by the therapist, a group of people with similar problems in an institution (for example a hospital or a prison), a family or even a self-help group. As with individual therapies there are many different types of group therapy.

One of the main reasons why group therapy has increased in popularity is a recognition that many psychological problems are associated with problems in dealing with other people. Therefore, providing a setting in which the problems can be worked out with other people is an important alternative to individual therapy.

see also...

*Anxiety; Clinical Psychology;
Depression; Freud, Sigmund;
Psychodynamic Approaches;
Schizophrenia*

Quantitative and Qualitative

John has just found out that his company is closing down the factory where he works. John and many other workers will be unemployed at the end of the week. What effect will this change in status have on the workers and their families? The impact unemployment has on the well-being of individuals and their families is an issue that has concerned psychologists throughout the twentieth century. But what kind of information could be collected to develop a better understanding of their experiences?

Within psychology it is possible to identify two major approaches to data collection – quantitative and qualitative. The quantitative approach is concerned with converting information into numerical data. An example of this approach would be a questionnaire or survey which asks people to indicate the extent to which they agree or disagree with specific statements. Responses can then be converted into a score which represents a person's views. One advantage of a quantitative approach is that it enables hypotheses to be tested and allows for easy comparison between different groups such as employed and unemployed people. A major criticism of the quantitative approach is that what people actually say can get lost when the data is converted into numbers.

Qualitative research is concerned with retaining the richness and variety of people's feelings and ideas. Interviews are widely used in qualitative research, but one important issue is what is done with the data after it has been collected, since interview data can easily be converted into numbers. For example, in an interview with John you could count the number of times he used words associated with depression as an indication of his mental well-being. However, a qualitative analysis of the interview would be concerned with the meanings John placed on the experience of becoming unemployed. Qualitative methodology examines the links between events and activities and explores people's interpretations of what underlies these links.

see also...

Correlation; Ethics; Experimental Method; Significance Testing; Survey

Reading

There are a number of processes involved in extracting the meaning from words printed on a page. As we read, our eyes are continually making rapid movements from one point on the page to another. These rapid movements are called saccades and each one lasts about 15 milliseconds. Following each saccade our eyes remain fixated on one point for approximately 250 milliseconds before the next saccade. It is only during the times when our eyes are stationary that we can extract information from the page.

One of the reasons why our eyes move around the page is to ensure that the words we are interested in are in the centre of our visual field, where our vision is at its most acute. Identifying and recognizing the words on a page requires that we process information at three different levels. We need to process information about the straight and curved lines on the page and we can use that information to identify the individual letters in the word. Once we have identified the individual letters we can identify the whole word. However, this is a very complex process and it is unlikely that it progresses in a simple sequence from shape to letter to word. It is much more likely that the process is interactive with features of the whole word influencing the recognition of individual letters as well as individual letters helping us to recognize the word.

One of the central concepts in word recognition and reading is the notion of a mental lexicon. Our mental lexicon contains all our knowledge about words, including their meaning, pronunciation and the role they play in sentences. We access this lexicon every time we read a word, but how do we access the correct word so quickly and efficiently? One suggestion is that people can recognize a word directly from the printed letters. In other words when we look at the word 'simple', recognizing the visual pattern is sufficient to access the meaning of the word in our lexicon.

see also...

Chomsky, Noam; Cognitive Psychology; Dyslexia; Language Development

Reliability and Validity

Amy's parents are a little concerned that her reading skills don't match her ability with numbers. After a discussion with her teacher they arrange for Amy to be seen by a psychologist. The psychologist gives Amy a psychological test that aims to assess her reading ability. After the test the psychologist tells Amy's parents that she scored 75 out of 130 which is about average for a girl of her age. How confident can Amy's parents be that the test score accurately reflects Amy's reading ability?

When assessing any measuring instrument, whether it is a psychological test or a thermometer, there are two issues that are vitally important – reliability and validity. Reliability is a measure of the extent to which the instrument will give the same reading when measuring the same thing on different occasions. Imagine you bought a thermometer and decided to test its accuracy by checking the reading it gives for boiling water. On Tuesday you place it in a pan of boiling water and it gives a reading of 100°C. You are happy that you have spent your money

wisely. However, if you repeat the test on Wednesday and get a reading of 92°C, and again on Thursday and get a reading of 127°C, you would not be happy. The same rationale applies to psychological tests. If the reading test Amy completed is reliable, then if she did it again in a couple of days time her score should be very close to 75. If the test is reliable then peoples' scores should be similar each time they take the test.

We also expect the test to be valid and measure what it is claiming to measure. In Amy's case, the test should really be measuring reading ability and not something else. Another aspect of validity concerns the extent to which performance on the test enables you to predict future performance – predictive validity. This is especially important in situations where psychological tests are being used to select people for particular jobs.

see also...

Correlation; Intelligence Quotient; Personality; Psychological Tests; Work and Organizational Psychology

Repression

The concept of repression is central to Freud's theory of psychoanalysis. Repression describes the process by which threatening and anxiety-provoking thoughts are denied access to conscious awareness. Since this process is said to operate at the unconscious level, a person would not be aware that he or she was repressing something.

Repression is one of the defence mechanisms proposed by Freud that operates to protect people from unpleasant thoughts and feelings. In Freud's view the repressed information is not lost but is stored in the unconscious from where it may surface at some point in the future. The repressed memory doesn't simply lay dormant but continues to exert an influence which may manifest itself through the content of dreams or, if the memory is especially traumatic, in some form of neurosis. Joan is a 30-year-old woman who is having problems with physical intimacy in her relationships. After several sessions with a therapist it emerged that she had been sexually abused by an uncle when she was a child. Prior to therapy Joan had no recollection of the abuse. In Freud's terminology, the memory of the abuse had been repressed but was manifesting itself through the problems Joan was experiencing with intimacy.

Freud believed that many of the slips of the tongue we make are the result of repressed information in our unconscious exerting an influence. For example, when Mustapha, a keen and competitive golfer, was introduced to a new member of the golf club he said, 'Pleased to beat you,' when in fact he had intended to say, 'Pleased to meet you'. This type of error is still referred to as a 'Freudian slip'.

There have been numerous attempts to investigate repression using an experimental approach. Some of these studies claim to provide support for Freud's theory of repression whereas others report little or no support for the idea.

see also...

Defence Mechanisms; Freud, Sigmund; False Memories; Memory; Psychodynamic Approaches

Schemas and Scripts

How do we make sense of stories and events we experience in our everyday lives? How do we know what to do when we go to a restaurant for a meal? Frederick Bartlett working in the first half of the twentieth century used the term 'schema' to refer to our organized patterns of knowledge about the world.

One of the topics that interested Bartlett was the way in which people remember stories. In order to investigate this he presented stories from different cultures to his students and then asked them to recall the stories. As you might expect, when people were asked to remember the stories after a period of time their recall was incomplete and contained errors. However, one of the striking observations made by Bartlett was not that people made errors, but rather that the errors people were making were heavily influenced by their own view of the world. When people are faced with a novel situation they use their existing schemas to try to interpret and make sense of the situation. One of Bartlett's major contributions to our understanding of memory processes was to develop the view that remembering the past is an active process of reconstruction.

More recently, Roger Schank and Robert Abelson have used the term 'script' to refer to our knowledge about the expected series of actions in everyday settings. For example, they developed a detailed account of a restaurant script which embodies our knowledge of the sequence of events and actions involved in a typical visit to a restaurant. Scripts are a particular kind of schema. The actions in a script are organized in terms of which actions must precede and follow certain other actions. For example, in a restaurant you must find a table before you sit down, and you sit down before you order. The actions in a script are also goal directed. In other words, you go to a restaurant for a purpose. It could be to satisfy your hunger or it could be part of a birthday celebration.

see also...

Cognitive Psychology; Episodic, Semantic and Procedural Memory; Impression Formation; Memory; Stereotypes

Schizophrenia

James believes that he is being spied on by the Russian secret police. He also believes that they are working in collaboration with other secret agencies around the world in an attempt to kill him because he knows where the alien spaceships are going to land. James is suffering from delusions, beliefs that have no basis in reality. Trying to hold a conversation with James is very difficult. His language is very disjointed and the subject of his conversation changes rapidly. Very often every sentence signals the start of another topic. Recently he has started to spend more and more time alone in his room or walking around on his own. James has been diagnosed as suffering from schizophrenia which is one of the most debilitating psychological disorders.

One of the problems encountered when attempting to diagnose schizophrenia is that no two cases are the same. There is no single symptom that characterises everybody who is suffering from schizophrenia. Symptoms of schizophrenia can be categorized into two groups. The first group includes delusions and hallucinations, such as hearing voices when no one is speaking. These symptoms are experiences outside the normal range of experiences. The second group of symptoms includes social withdrawal, apathy and a lack of interest in anything. These symptoms are the absence of behaviours normally expected of people.

It has been estimated that approximately one per cent of the population will experience schizophrenia at some point in their lives. It is most likely to occur in adolescence and early adulthood. Unlike many other mental health problems schizophrenia is treated primarily with drug therapy. About one-third of the people experiencing schizophrenia will make a good recovery; the others will either suffer repeated episodes or have prolonged periods of schizophrenia. It has also been estimated that approximately ten per cent of homeless people are schizophrenic.

see also...

Anxiety; Clinical Psychology; Depression; Neurotransmitters

Self-Efficacy

Tim and Ruth are physicians. Tim is always questioning his ability as a physician, whereas Ruth is very confident in her ability to diagnose medical problems and prescribe an effective and appropriate treatment. When Tim is faced by a difficult case he finds it extremely stressful and often delays making a diagnosis. On the other hand, Ruth copes well with difficult cases and doesn't find them any more stressful than the run-of-the-mill cases. Tim and Ruth have different levels of self-efficacy.

Self-efficacy is a concept developed by Albert Bandura and refers to a person's evaluation of their ability to cope well in a specific situation. Bandura is particularly interested in the relationship between self-efficacy and behaviour. In the case of Ruth and Tim, self-efficacy refers to their beliefs about their ability to carry out their job as a physician. A person's level of self-efficacy isn't constant, but varies according to different situations. For example, Tim might have little faith in his ability as a physician but his levels of self-efficacy might be high when it comes to activities such as skiing or playing the piano.

There are a number of factors which can affect a person's level of self-efficacy in any given situation. These include a person's previous experience of a situation. If Tim has been successful in the past, he is likely to have higher levels of self-efficacy than if he had failed. What other people say about a person's ability to cope with specific situations can also affect levels of self-efficacy. If they tell you that you have ability and skills to succeed it is likely to have a positive effect on your levels of self-efficacy. If levels of self-efficacy can be influenced by other people this suggests that they are not fixed. It has been suggested that certain phobias, for example a fear of snakes, can be viewed as a reaction involving low self-efficacy. In other words people are frightened because they lack confidence in their ability to cope with a snake. One of the forms of treating phobias involves helping people to develop confidence in their ability to cope effectively with the object of their phobia.

see also...

Anxiety; Bandura, Albert; Coping Strategies; Social Psychology; Stress

Significance Testing

Imagine the following scenario. Ten people have volunteered to take part in an experiment and we allocate them to either group A or group B by drawing their names out of a hat. The participants are timed to see how long it takes them to put some cubes into a box. The average time is calculated for each group. The average time for group A was 37.5 seconds and for group B the average time was 39.8 seconds. In a situation like this it is extremely likely that there will be a difference between the average times for each group. However, because the groups were selected randomly and they were completing the same task it is reasonable to assume that the difference between the groups occurred by chance.

Now consider the following situation. A researcher is interested in the effect of noise on performance, so she designs an experiment with two conditions. In the first condition participants have to complete a task in total silence. In the second condition participants have to complete exactly the same task, but the noise level is kept at a constant 55 decibels. When all the participants have completed the experiment the researcher calculates the average time it took to complete the task. In the first condition the average time was 127 seconds and in the second condition it was 143 seconds. How can we decide whether the difference between the two conditions was due to the noise or to chance differences between the groups? Psychologists attempt to deal with this by using statistical techniques that calculate the probability of differences between the groups occurring by chance. If the likelihood of the difference between the results occurring by chance is less than five per cent then psychologists accept that the differences are due to the experimental manipulation rather than chance fluctuations. Psychologists refer to a difference between conditions that is not due to chance as a 'significant' difference.

see also...

Correlation; Ethics; Experimental Method; Quantitative and Qualitative; Reliability and Validity; Survey

Skinner, Burrhus Frederick

Burrhus Frederick Skinner (1903–90) was born and raised in the small rural town of Susquehanna, Pennsylvania. At college he majored in English Literature and aspired to be a writer. After graduating he spent an unsuccessful year trying to earn a living as a writer. Skinner was one of the best known proponents of the behaviourist approach in psychology. Behaviourists argue that because we have no direct access to another person's conscious and unconscious, psychology should focus on observable behaviours.

Skinner did much of his work with animals such as pigeons and rats. In order to study learning in the laboratory he developed a device which is now universally known as a 'Skinner box'. A Skinner box consists essentially of a box containing a lever attached to a food dispenser. If the lever is pressed a pellet of food is dropped into the box. Obviously, when rats or pigeons were first placed in the Skinner box they were unlikely to go and press the lever. In order to get the animals to do this, their behaviour was progressively shaped. This was a precise and meticulous process and was carried out by dropping food pellets into the cage whenever the animal approached the lever. Eventually this progressed to a stage when the animal would be rewarded only if it touched the lever, and finally it had to press the lever to get a reward. Using this technique Skinner had amazing success in teaching pigeons to perform complex tasks. During the Second World War he taught three pigeons to guide a missile. However, the project was abandoned in favour of the atom bomb.

One of Skinner's basic ideas was that our behaviour is determined by the environment. The term operant is used to refer to a behaviour that has some effect on the environment. For example, opening a door for someone, holding hands with your partner and asking for help, are all examples of operants.

see also...

Behaviour Modification; Behaviour Therapy; Behaviourism; Chomsky, Noam; Conditioning; Language Development

Sleep

It has been estimated that we spend approximately 30 per cent of our lives asleep. This means that if we live long enough to enjoy our seventieth birthday most of us will have spent about 21 years sleeping. Despite a vast amount of research into sleep there is still no agreement as to its function. One thing that is clear, however, is that being deprived of sleep has a number of unpleasant consequences. For example, after sleep deprivation the effectiveness of our immune system is reduced, making us susceptible to a range of diseases. In addition, people who stay awake for more than one night are extremely likely to experience hallucinations.

One device that has been used to investigate sleep is called an electroencephalograph, or EEG for short. This involves attaching a number of electrodes to different parts of the head which make it possible to monitor electrical activity in the brain. Using this technique it is possible to identify a number of different stages that take place during a normal night's sleep. The first stage signals the transition from a waking state to sleep and is accompanied by a reduction in heart rate and muscle tension. This stage is relatively brief and lasts only a few minutes. Once we are asleep we move through the different stages of sleep in a cycle which lasts about 90 minutes. Each cycle takes us through different levels of sleep from light sleep, when it is relatively easy to wake someone, through to deep sleep when it is rather more difficult to wake a person. In an average night's sleep we will go through this cycle five or six times. One of the stages in the cycle is characterized by rapid eye movements and is often referred to as REM sleep. As the night progresses the proportion of time spent in REM sleep during each cycle increases, so that in the couple of hours before waking the majority of time is spent in REM sleep. Although it does seem to be the case that the majority of people do dream during REM sleep, it is not the only time that we dream – people dream in other stages of sleep as well.

see also...

Biopsychology; Brain Structure; Dreams; Neurotransmitters

Social Development

During their early years children learn how to interact with others and develop relationships. They develop an understanding of how to behave in different social settings such school and the family home. Social development refers to the process of learning how to relate to others and developing as a person.

Social relationships begin almost as soon as a child is born and continue throughout a person's life. Erik Erikson proposed a theory of social development throughout the lifespan which identifies eight stages in the development of a person as a social being. The stages are referred to as psychosocial stages and during each stage people face a challenge, or developmental task, which is typical for that period of a person's life. According to Erikson, if people don't cope successfully with the challenges it can result in psychological problems.

The first stage comprises the first 18 months of life and is concerned with the extent to which infants are able to develop a sense of trust in others. The second stage takes place when children are two or three years old. It is at this stage that children are developing a sense of autonomy and a view of themselves as independent individuals. Between the ages of seven and 11 years, children begin to compare themselves to other children in terms of their abilities, clothes, popularity and so on. Erikson saw the next stage, adolescence, as a time when individuals develop a sense of identity. After adolescence comes the stage of early adulthood where the developmental task is the establishment of long-lasting relationships. Erikson saw the challenge of middle age as one of producing something of lasting value to society. The final stage is old age when Erikson suggested that individuals can look back on their lives either with a sense of satisfaction at having lived it well or a sense of despair and regret.

see also...

Adolescence; Attachment; Cognitive Development; Developmental Psychology; Social Psychology

Social Facilitation

onsider the following situation. You are at home putting up some shelves and someone else comes into the room where you are working. Will the presence of another person have any effect on your performance? This was the question Norman Triplett investigated in 1897 in one of the earliest psychology experiments. He looked at how quickly children turned a fishing reel under different conditions. In some conditions they were on their own and in others they performed the task in the same room as other children. Triplett reported that the children worked faster when another child doing the same task was present than when they worked alone.

Subsequent studies using different tasks, such as multiplication problems, confirmed Triplett's findings. However, it soon became apparent that it wasn't necessary for the other people present to be doing the same task. The mere presence of other people appeared to have a beneficial effect on performance. This effect has been called social facilitation. Interestingly, social facilitation can also be observed in animals. For example, cockroaches run faster to escape a bright light if they are in pairs rather than alone!

Other research has reported that the presence of other people sometimes had a negative effect on performance. How can we explain these contradictory findings? One explanation suggests that the mere presence of others raises our general level of arousal. A consequence of this increase in our arousal levels is that we perform easy tasks, or tasks we are familiar with, better than difficult or unfamiliar tasks. A second explanation suggests that it is not the mere presence of others that raises our general level of arousal but rather individuals' concerns about being evaluated. In studies where the participants' concerns about being evaluated have been alleviated (for example, by blindfolding the audience) the social facilitation effect has been considerably reduced.

see also...

Groups; Pro-Social Behaviour; Social Psychology; Sport Psychology; Work and Organizational Psychology

Social Psychology

Why are we attracted to some people and not others? Why do some people discriminate against others? What are the factors that influence a person's aggressive behaviour? Are true leaders born and not made? These are some of the questions that are addressed in social psychology. Social psychology is concerned with understanding the factors that influence how we think and act in social situations.

Although there are many factors which can play a role in determining our social behaviour, many of them fall into three broad categories described below. First, the behaviour and characteristics of other people can have a significant impact on the way we behave. For example, a behaviour such as queue jumping is likely to elicit an unfavourable response from other people in the queue. In addition, people's physical appearance and dress can have a strong influence on how other people treat them. Second, the way in which we interpret and think about events and situations can play an important role in determining our behaviour in social settings. For example, if you

are in hospital for a routine operation and your friend has promised to visit you but doesn't arrive, you are likely to be really annoyed and upset at being let down like this. Later, when you are at home convalescing your friend comes to the house and apologizes for not visiting you in hospital. She tells you that her mother became ill very suddenly and she had to go and look after her. How do you react? The way your friend has behaved in the past could have an important influence on your reaction. If your friend has been totally reliable in the past then you are more likely to be understanding than if she has repeatedly let you down in lots of different situations. In other words, your knowledge and memory of past behaviours is playing an important role in your current behaviour. A third factor that can have a major influence on a person's behaviour is the cultural context.

> ## see also...
>
> *Aggression; Interpersonal Attraction; Intimate Relationships; Prejudice; Pro-Social Behaviour; Social Facilitation, Stereotypes*

Sport Psychology

In practice Michelle could shoot the basketball through the hoop from almost anywhere, but when it came to a game it was a different story. If the team was winning easily it was not a problem, but if it was a close game Michelle did not seem able to cope with the pressure and missed a lot of easy shots. Michelle's performance meant that the team was losing a lot of games by narrow margins. Her team mates also recognized the problem and in close games tended to stop passing to Michelle. The situation got so bad that Michelle was thinking about giving up basketball altogether. Eventually the coach contacted a sport psychologist to see if she could help.

Sport psychologists consult with individuals or teams to help athletes optimize their performance. In Michelle's case a sport psychologist would probably begin by talking to her and asking what she felt the differences were between practice and competitive games. It is likely that Michelle suffers from some form of competitive anxiety which affects her concentration during games. There are a number of techniques that can be used to help Michelle overcome her anxiety in games including relaxation exercises and visualization techniques. The role of the sport psychologist doesn't just cover working with the individual athlete since the behaviour of other team members and the coach could be influencing Michelle's levels of anxiety. For example, if the coach consistently stresses to Michelle how important the game is and how important her contribution is to the team it is likely to increase her levels of anxiety and have a detrimental effect on her performance.

Sport psychology is a relatively new area of interest within psychology, but it is also an area of rapid growth. In 1976 the United States Olympic Committee assigned a psychologist to be with its athletes for the first time. By 1984 psychological services were routinely provided to United States team members. Today, most athletes recognize that their mental approach to their sport can be improved with the help of a sport psychologist.

see also...

Anxiety; Emotion; Health Psychology; Parapsychology

Stereotypes

Imagine that you were asked to make a list of the characteristics of the following groups: Americans, Irish, English, women, men, homosexuals, vegetarians, homeless people and psychologists. You would probably be able to make a list for each group, even in cases where you have had no personal contact with members of the group. We all tend to hold beliefs about different social groups, and in many cases we believe that all members of a particular social group share similar characteristics and traits. These beliefs are called stereotypes.

Stereotypes can be brought to mind very easily and exert a considerable effect on how we interpret situations and information. For example, when we are presented with information that is inconsistent with our stereotypes, we add to it and interpret it in such a way that it becomes consistent with our stereotypes. Consider the following sentence: 'The student was unhappy about the amount of alcohol available at the party.' We make judgements about the information in the sentence based on our stereotype of students. If our stereotype of students is that they enjoy drinking and partying we would come to the conclusion that the reason the student was unhappy was because there wasn't sufficient alcohol available. On the other hand, if the person making the statement was a nun, we would probably conclude that she was concerned that there was too much alcohol. In some situations stereotypes, particularly negative stereotypes, can lead to prejudice. However, in other situations having certain stereotypes helps us make sense of a complex world.

It has been suggested that stereotypes operate as a labour saving device for our mental processes. When we meet people for the first time, stereotypes can help us to predict how they are likely to behave and adjust our own behaviour accordingly. When we describe members of other social groups we tend to emphasize their similarity to each other. For example, how many times have you heard a woman say, 'Men, they're all the same!'

see also...

Attitudes; Impression Formation; Prejudice; Schemas and Scripts; Social Psychology

Stress

Mr Smith is a teacher. He has been having problems with a group of adolescent boys in one of his classes. They spend most of their time talking and messing about. When Mr Smith challenges them they are usually rude and in the last class one of the group threatened to damage Mr Smith's car. Mr Smith can't stop thinking about the incident and how he is going to handle the group next time he has to teach them. He is finding it difficult to concentrate and even though he is tired, finds it difficult to get to sleep at night. When Mr Smith is driving to school his hands start to feel clammy and his heart pounds against his chest and all he can think about is having to teach that group of boys. A couple of days later Mr Smith decides he needs some time off work and he stays at home for the rest of the week.

We frequently use the word stress, but often use it in a fairly vague way. Using Mr Smith's situation we can identify four major kinds of effects that are associated with being stressed. First, emotional effects, such as feeling anxious and tense. Second, physiological effects such as increased heart rate and reduced appetite. Third, cognitive effects, such as poor concentration and increased distractibility. Fourth, behavioural effects, such as disrupted sleep patterns and increased absenteeism. But what causes stress? The transactional model of stress suggests that stress occurs when an individual believes that they do not have the ability to handle the demands of a situation. So Mr Smith's stress arose out of his perceived inability to cope with the boys in his class.

Long-term exposure to stressful situations can result in a range of physical symptoms including heart disease, damage to the body's immune system and stomach ulcers. The different ways people use to cope with stress are called coping strategies. The effectiveness of coping strategies depends on the situation, with some being better suited to situations than others.

see also...

Biopsychology; Coping Strategies; Health Psychology; Job Satisfaction; Sleep; Work and Organizational Psychology

Survey

Saimah was walking along the street when a person with a clipboard approached her and said, 'Have you got a couple of minutes to answer some questions for me?' Saimah was being asked to participate in a survey. Most people reading this book will have participated in a survey at some time or other. Surveys are used widely to investigate phenomena, such as the preferences of consumers, views of political parties and intended voting behaviour. Survey research in psychology typically involves asking large numbers of people questions about their attitudes and behaviour. Information is usually collected either by questionnaires, which people complete by themselves, or by interviews in which questions are asked in a standard format. Selecting the sample of people to be included in the survey is extremely important since it needs to be representative of the population. Random selection is a technique frequently used to identify a sample to be included in a survey. A researcher who wants a sample of residents from London could randomly select names from the electoral register.

In some types of research it is important that the sample accurately reflects certain characteristics of the whole population, such as age or socio-economic status. A technique called 'stratified random sampling' aims to do this by specifying the percentage of people to be drawn from each category. For example, in the case of age, you would specify the percentage of the sample in each age group based on the distribution of ages in the total population. So, if 25 per cent of the whole population was aged between 65 and 75, then 25 per cent of the sample would need to be aged between 65 and 75. This would ensure that the age distribution of the sample selected for the survey was an accurate reflection of the age distribution in the whole population.

One of the major problems with surveys is the fact that they rely on participants' ability to report on their own behaviour.

see also...

Attitudes; Correlation; Ethics;
Experimental Method;
Quantitative and Qualitative;
Reliability and Validity

Work and Organizational Psychology

Charles O'Regan is the Managing Director of a company employing 300 people. He wants to change the structure of his sales force. This will involve promoting some of the existing sales staff to area managers and employing more sales personnel. How can Charles ensure that he promotes the most appropriate people, and how can he ensure that the new sales personnel are going to generate the new business the company needs?

Designing new personnel selection procedures is one of the tasks that would fall within the remit of a work and organizational psychologist. One of the main goals in personnel selection is to provide an estimate of a person's future job performance. Ideally the design of a selection process should begin with a systemic analysis of the job in order to determine the qualities necessary to perform effectively. The next stage would involve the identification of appropriate selection procedures that would aim to assess the extent to which candidates had the qualities appropriate to the job. These procedures could include techniques that attempt to sample tasks which people actually perform in the job. For example, the potential area managers could be presented with a simulation in which they are asked to prioritize a set of tasks. Other techniques rely on the measurement of psychological qualities such as intelligence or personality that are thought to be predictive of job success. But work and organizational psychology encompasses many more issues than just personnel selection and in its broadest sense it is concerned with applying psychological principles to people's work. This includes the development of training programmes and stress management.

Different countries have adopted slightly different terms to describe this area of psychology. For example, the terms industrial psychology, occupational psychology, the psychology of work and organizations and industrial/organizational psychology are all used fairly widely.

see also...

Health Psychology; Job Satisfaction; Stress; Psychological Tests

Further Reading

If you are looking for a book that provides you with an overview of the main areas of psychology try one of the following:

Eysenck, M.W. (ed) *Psychology: an integrated approach*, Harlow: Addison Wesley Longman, 1998

Gray, P, *Psychology*, New York: Worth Publishers, 1999

Scott, P. & Spencer, C. (eds) *Psychology: a contemporary introduction*, Oxford: Blackwell, 1998

Sternberg, R.J., *In search of the human mind*, Fort Worth: Harcourt Brace, 1995

Westen, D., *Psychology: mind, brain & culture*, New York: John Wiley & Sons, 1999

If you want to read something that focuses on a specific topic within psychology then the following list might provide a useful starting point:

Arrigo, B.A., *Introduction to forensic psychology*, London: Academic Press, 1999

Baddeley, A.D., *Essentials of memory*, Hove: Psychology Press, 1999

Bentley, E., *Awareness: biorhythms, sleep & dreaming*, London: Routledge, 1999

Brannigan, G.G., *Experiencing psychology: active learning adventures*, Engelwood Cliffs, N.J.: Prentice Hall, 1999

Chmiel, N., *Introduction to work & organized psychology*, Oxford: Blackwell, 1999

Clamp, A. & Russell, J., *Comparative psychology*, London: Hodder & Stoughton, 1998

Curtis, A., *Health psychology*, London: Routledge, 1999

Evans, D., *Introducing evolutionary psychology*, Cambridge: Icon Books, 1999

Eysenck, M.W., *Principles of cognitive psychology*, Hove: Psychology Press, 1993

Feldman, R.S., *Development across the lifespan*, Englewood Cliffs, N.J.: Prentice Hall, 1999

Ferris, P., *Dr. Freud: a life*, Washington, DC: Counterpoint Press, 1999

Fordham, F., *An introduction to Jung's psychology*, Harmondsworth: Penguin, 1991

Gross, R. & McIlveen, R., *Perspective in psychology*, London: Hodder & Stoughton, 1999

Harrower, J., *Applying psychology to crime*, London: Hodder & Stoughton, 1998

Heffernan, T.M., *A student's guide to studying psychology*, Hove: Psychology Press, 1997

Jarvis, M., *Sport psychology*, London: Routledge, 1999

Kalat, J.W., *Biological psychology*, Pacific Grove, CA: Brooks/Cole, 1998

Lemma-Wright, A., *Invitation to psychodynamic psychology*, London: Whurr
    Publishers, 1995

Matlin, M., *Psychology of women*, Fort Worth: Harcourt Brace, 1999

Nunn, J. (ed) *Laboratory psychology*, Hove: Psychology Press, 1997

Pennington, D., Gillen, K. & Hill, P., *Social psychology*, London: Arnold, 1999

Pinel, J.P.J. & Edwards, M.E., *Colorful introduction to the anatomy of the human
    brain, A: A brain and psychology coloring book*, New York: Prentice Hall, 1997

Shattler, D.N., Shabatay, V. & Kramer, G.P., *Abnormal psychology in context*,
    Boston: Houghton Mifflin, 1998

Trew, K. & Kremer, J., *Gender & psychology*, London: Arnold, 1998

Vasta, R., *Child psychology: a student's guide*, New York: John Wiley & Sons,
    1998

Also available in the series